Color Your Cloth

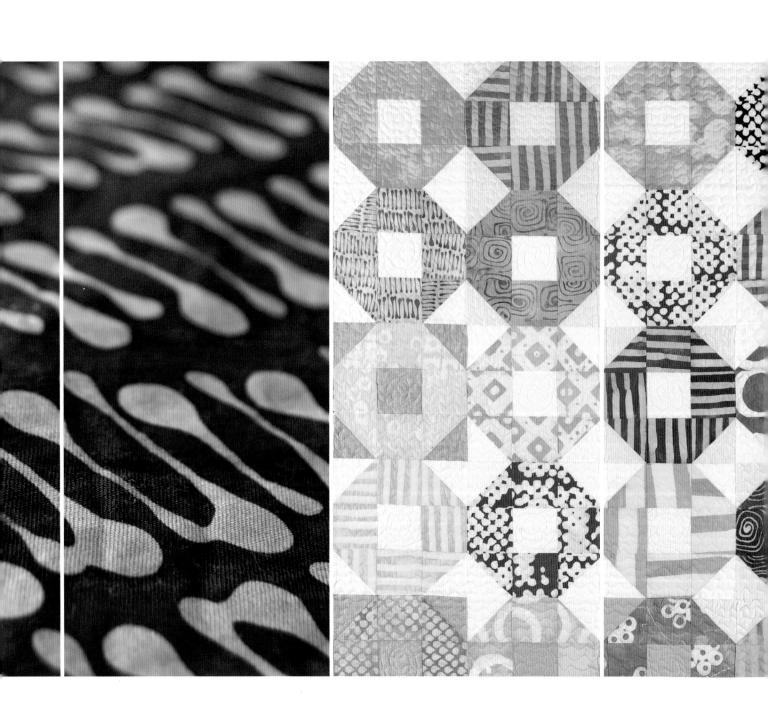

Color Your Cloth

A Quilter's Guide to Dyeing and Patterning Fabric

Malka Dubrawsky

LARK BOOKS

A Division of Sterling Publishing Co., Inc.

New York / London

Library of Congress Cataloging-in-Publication Data

Dubrawsky, Malka.
 Color your cloth : a quilter's guide to dyeing and patterning fabric / Malka
Dubrawsky. -- 1st ed.
    p. cm.
 Includes index.
 ISBN 978-1-60059-513-4 (pb-pbk. with flaps : alk. paper)
 1. Dyes and dyeing, Domestic. 2. Dyes and dyeing--Textile fibers. I.
Title.
 TT853.D84 2009
 648'.1--dc22

                              2009014895

10 9 8 7 6 5 4 3 2 1

First Edition

A Red Lips 4 Courage
Communications, Inc. book
www.redlips4courage.com
Eileen Cannon Paulin
    President
Catherine Risling
    Director of Editorial
Erika Kotite
    Developmental Director

Senior Editor:
    Darra Williamson
Copy Editors:
    Mary Beth Adomitas
    Catherine Risling
Art Director:
    Susan H. Hartman
Illustrator:
    Tim Manibusan
Photographers:
    Gregory Case
    Malka Dubrawsky

Published by Lark Books, A Division of
Sterling Publishing Co., Inc.
387 Park Ave. South, New York, NY 10016

Text © 2009, Malka Dubrawsky
Photography © 2009, Red Lips 4 Courage Communications, Inc.
Illustrations © 2009, Red Lips 4 Courage Communications, Inc.

Distributed in Canada by Sterling Publishing,
c/o Canadian Manda Group, 165 Dufferin St.
Toronto, Ontario, Canada M6K 3H6

Distributed in the United Kingdom by GMC Distribution Services,
Castle Place, 166 High St., Lewes, East Sussex, England BN7 1XU

Distributed in Australia by Capricorn Link (Australia) Pty Ltd.,
P.O. Box 704, Windsor, NSW 2756 Australia

If you have questions or comments about this book, please contact:

Lark Books
67 Broadway
Asheville, NC 28801
(828) 253-0467

Manufactured in China

ISBN 13: 978-1-60059-513-4

For information about custom editions, special sales, premium and corporate purchases, please
contact Sterling Special Sales Department at (800) 805-5489 or specialsales@sterlingpub.com.

Dedication

I'm fortunate to come from a family with
a strong crafting tradition; I don't think I
would value the handmade as much as I do
if it hadn't been for the wonderful example
set by my mother, Nechama Dubrawsky, my
aunt, Tova Kleinmann, and my grandmother,
Zehava Bernstein.

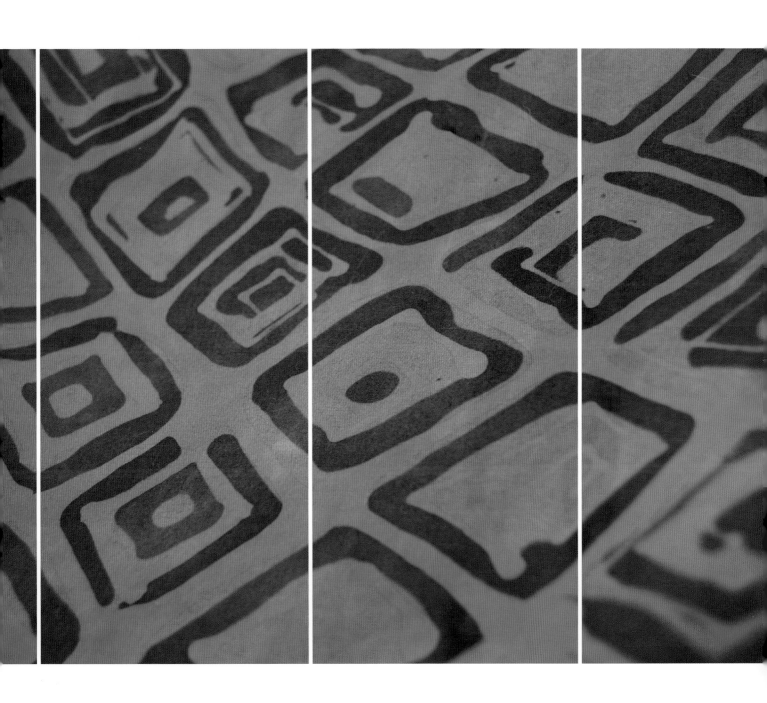

Contents

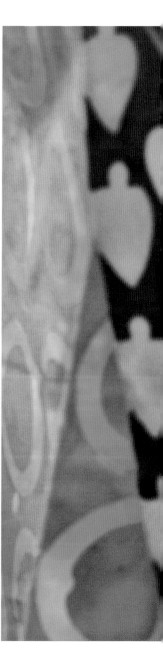

An Introduction to the Process

I haven't been the same since Mrs. Stapleton's eighth-grade art class introduced me to the process of applying wax to fabric. Even though I went on to get an art degree that focused on printmaking, I never forgot the way we melted wax in muffin tins, painted that wax onto fabric, and then taped our completed batik fabrics to the classroom window so that we could see them backlit by the sun. It made a big impression on me, despite the fact that I registered for art class only to get out of taking physical education.

Being at home with children prompted my second encounter with the batik (or wax-resist) process. Though I had a space for making art at home, it was completely impractical for the kind of printmaking I had learned in college. I'd been gravitating toward sewing and quilting, but there seemed to be something missing. I soon discovered that patterning and dyeing my own fabric was that missing link. It reminded me of everything I loved about printmaking, especially the multiplicity of processes. But, unlike printmaking, where all the wonderful techniques happened on my

printing plate and seemed to flatten when I transferred the image onto paper, with batik, the process and product existed in the finished piece of fabric.

That realization changed everything and prompted me to experiment with a variety of surface-design techniques. I also started to make my quilts exclusively with my own fabrics.

For several years, I used those fabrics to make art quilts, but after a while, I came to feel that once again something was missing. As much as I enjoyed the "in-my-head" interaction that making these quilts brought me, I craved a more tangible connection. I couldn't help but think back to the times I had made a gift for someone from my own hand-dyed fabrics. The recipient was always so touched by the extra effort and thought that went into crafting something for them from "start to finish." I'd liken the experience to knitting a pair of mittens with your own handspun yarn; I knew that making items from my own fabrics that were both useful and beautiful would bring me that kind of connection.

The concept of sewing for ourselves and for others is not a recent phenomenon, but I think that a newly discovered passion for all things DIY (do-it-yourself) has fueled a new generation of stitchers to take up needle and thread. These "newbies," as well as those who have been sewing for years, are eager to learn new techniques in their quest to put something of themselves into everything they make.

Happily for me, this desire affords me another opportunity to make connections by teaching *you* how to pattern and dye your own fabric—in this case, with batik or wax resist—and how to fashion that fabric into fun and functional objects.

There are many ways to apply resists to fabric, but they all have the same goal: to *prevent* dye from coloring certain parts of a piece of fabric. In the processes described in the following chapters, the resist medium is melted wax. With its application, you can control what parts of the fabric get colored and how.

In discussing batik, I'll also walk you through the process of mixing your own dye baths using fiber-reactive, cold-water dyes.

These wonderfully intense, transparent dyes are ideal for the wax-resist method because they don't require heating and won't melt the wax. They're very easy and safe to work with and make creating a rainbow of colors just a matter of following a simple recipe.

The beauty of the process I describe in this book is that it adjusts to your level of knowledge and interest in experimentation. Whether you're passionate about creating simple graphic patterns or want to combine and layer techniques, this method is right for you. For instance, discharging, or bleaching, is a technique that can be used alone or combined with other processes to create a more complex surface design. Additionally, overdyeing—or adding a second, third, or fourth layer of dye—allows you to put color back, add more color, and generally add intensity to your fabric surface.

It really takes crafting to a whole new level when you make the creative decisions for both the final product and the materials used. You might see it as an extra bit of control over the finished item, but I like to think of it as another opportunity to put something of yourself into everything you sew.

Chapter 1

Finding Inspiration

The best thing about a life drawing class is the predetermined subject matter: the human form, often a nude. Without the anxiety of trying to decide what to draw, you can focus on *how* you want to draw and with what materials.

This is not the case in patterning fabric. You might have a repertoire of processes, but you still have to figure out what image or pattern you want to apply to your fabric. While this may prompt some concern, it really is an opportunity to train your eyes to seek inspiration in the patterns and colors that are omnipresent in our world.

Recording Your Ideas

The first step in becoming aware of the everyday inspirations that surround you is to get a sketchbook or journal. If your first reaction to this suggestion is to crinkle your nose as you decry your drawing skills, my response is: *You don't have to draw.* I've been keeping sketchbooks for almost 20 years, and although there are sketches in these journals, there are even more magazine tearsheets, photographs, pressed leaves, package labels, and other ephemera and miscellany. If I'm flipping through a store catalog and I notice an interesting pattern on the marked-for-clearance couch, I tear out that picture and add it to my sketchbook.

My sketchbooks have been an invaluable resource for patterning inspiration.

If I purchase a skein of yarn because I fell in love with the color, I add a strand or two to my sketchbook; if I really like the colors and layout of the yarn label, I add that as well. My philosophy is that if it captures my eye, even momentarily, it's worth adding to my sketchbook. I can always edit the pages later, but I never want to recall an image or color combination and wish I had taken the time to include it.

Along with collecting magazine and newspaper images, I also take, print, and store my own photographs in my sketchbooks. I'm often struck by a pattern or color and want to have a visual record of it. Taking my own pictures and adding those to a journal is a great way to expand my library of inspirations.

Look Everywhere

Having solved the issue of organizing your images, the next step is deciding where to look for inspiration. My simple response is, "Look everywhere!" However, if I examine where most of my inspiration comes from, I'd have to narrow it down to four sources: architecture, nature, collections of everyday items, and other art, especially textiles.

Step outside and look at the buildings around you. In a community or city with a true downtown, it doesn't take much searching to find patterns created by the intersection of steel supports and the placement of windows. Look closely at the brick or ironwork used to adorn houses in your neighborhood. Take note of the colors of the houses, both individually and as a group. If you happen to live on a wide plateau in the middle of nowhere, then let the post office deliver your architectural inspiration. Home and garden magazines are a great source of amazing images of buildings and other structures, both new and old.

Architectural elements are a great source of inspiration for patterning your own fabrics.

No matter where you live, you can find pattern and color inspiration in nature. Years ago, struck by the orange cosmos flowers and lavender that were—by happenstance—growing side by side in my garden, I dyed fabrics for a quilt in shades of orange and pale purple. I cursed the banana tree that my daughter begged me to plant until the day I took the time to photograph its leaves up close. In browsing through my old sketchbooks, I was a little surprised to see how many different examples of leaf shapes I'd recorded, either by pressing the leaves into the book or by photograph. For me, the shapes and forms found in the natural world are a wonderful source of abstract patterns.

Nature abounds with inspirational shapes, colors, and textures.

Even the most familiar of everyday objects, or the most humble of collections, can spark your imagination.

Another much-relied on resource is my collection of what could best be described as the "detritus of everyday life." I have an affinity for groupings of things. Ideally, those things would be diamonds, but since I don't have that kind of budget, I settle for the beauty in a bowl of empty spools or collected corks. A massing of same, simple objects can reveal rich new patterns. If you're skeptical, take time to look carefully at a bowl of buttons or a bundle of twigs. A large grouping of a single object shows both the form of that object and the space around it. There's quite a visual treasure to be culled from a mundane collection.

Probably my greatest source of inspiration comes from other works of art. Whether the art form is Native American pottery or Bauhaus weavings, I constantly find myself returning to books featuring these images. I particularly love textiles from other cultures, such as Kuba cloths from Zaire and Ralli quilts from India. These works can provide color, texture, and pattern inspiration, often in a single piece. I might choose to mimic the diamond pattern of Kuba cloths, or the intense reds, yellows, and oranges of Indian embroidery. *You* might be inspired by something I've never even noticed, and create patterning based on that source. No matter what culture the art comes from, its style, or the technique used to create it, a world of inspiration exists at your fingertips with a visit to your local library, bookstore, or museum.

Explore other artwork, including ethnic textiles and work in other media, for patterning inspiration.

A contemporary corollary to the available wealth of inspiration is the Internet. I couldn't possibly discuss what stirs my creative juices without mentioning the World Wide Web. Before the availability of online photo-sharing sites such as Flickr, I often felt as though my eyes were literally "hungry" for new images. Though I've wasted my fair share of time surfing the Web, I honestly feel that what I've lost in spare moments has been compensated for with images that made me sigh with awe or delight, or that allowed me to see something from a fresh perspective. I consider the Internet an invaluable tool, providing a wonderful opportunity to be inspired.

As you train yourself to become more observant, I think you'll find that inspiration is not that elusive. The suggestions I've made here may be all you need to get your creative juices flowing, or to spark your curiosity to look in other places and compile a list of patterning sources that are unique to you.

Chapter 2

Creating a Workspace

One of the reasons I decided to write this book—other than just plain loving the process—is the adaptability of my particular method for home use. Like most people, I don't have a separate studio space overlooking a beautiful vista, complete with assistant. I must carve my workspace out of my living space, and the way I work must mesh with my family and my home life. I know this process can be done in a home setting because I *do* it in a home setting. So can you!

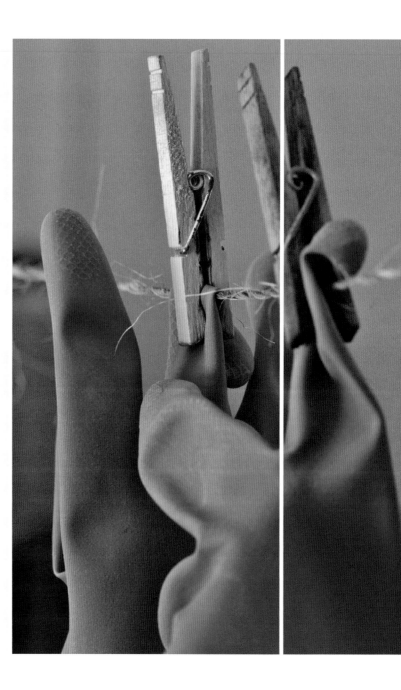

You don't need a fancy studio for dyeing and waxing. A corner of my garage serves as my primary workspace.

Finding a Space

Where to set up your workspace is an important consideration. Since both the dyeing and waxing techniques I use require good ventilation, a garage or covered porch is ideal. One of the advantages of working in this type of space is that drips and spills won't be a problem. My own space is tucked into a corner of my garage, and includes a few shelves to store materials, two tables, and a makeshift clothesline for hanging fabric inside when it's raining. All this, and we still manage to park the car there. As an added boon, I find that my car makes a wonderful temporary spot for laying out my fabrics in progress.

In addition to good ventilation, you'll need access to electricity, even if that means running an extension cord, and access to water from a nearby tap or garden hose.

Ideally your space would include at least one large table that can do double duty for both waxing and dyeing. No matter how careful you are, this table will get stained, so please don't use the antique mahogany table you inherited. A cheap but sturdy thrift-store find is your best bet, and you'll probably want to use a protective covering—for example, a large piece of cardboard—for splashes, drips, and spills. You'll also want some storage for items such as soda ash, bleach, and extra blocks of wax. (More on this in later chapters.) If you're working on a porch, and need your materials to be portable, store them in a large plastic box and bring them out when needed. The only materials that must be stored indoors are your dyes. They'll last much longer if they're not exposed to temperature changes.

Stocking Your Space

After moving the kids' bikes to make room for your worktable, you'll need to equip your space with a few essentials. First and foremost you'll need a temperature-controlled electric frying pan. For the sake of safety, this is a non-negotiable item. A temperature-controlled electric frying pan allows you to heat the wax safely. When turned on, it is your source for melted wax. When you're done, simply unplug the pan and allow the wax to cool and harden; this same pan stores that wax for future use.

Another must-have is a large cardboard box with the top removed or folded in. This will function as your frame for stretching fabric for patterning. Eventually this box will wear out. At that point, recycle it and buy yourself something else that comes in a large cardboard box.

Like the temperature-controlled frying pan, a quality respirator or dust mask and rubber gloves are key. These items ensure that this fun process remains a safe process as well. You won't need the gloves and respirator when you're working with the wax, but once you're ready to mix up a dye bath, you'll want to have them both handy.

Other workspace necessities include:

- Apron
- Dishpan
- Fiber-reactive, cold-water dyes
- Kitchen scale for weighing wax
- Measuring cups and spoons
- One gallon (3.8 liters) calibrated bucket or pitcher
- Small plastic containers for mixing dyes
- Stamping tools and brushes
- Tacks or pushpins
- Wax

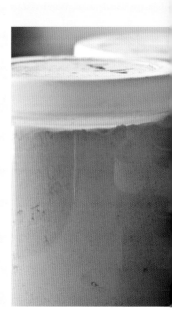

Chapter 3

Techniques for Adding Pattern to Fabric

As passionate as I am about color, especially the color orange, I'm even more interested in how a given pattern can alter the look of a fabric. The "feel" of a fabric can change completely depending upon the type of imagery that adorns its surface. For instance, large, simple, evenly spaced shapes give a fabric a graphic—possibly even retro—look, while clusters of delicate flowers suggest softness and femininity. It's all about "what's on top," and batik allows you to craft fabrics with a wide range of patterning.

Simple Processes, Accessible Tools

The batiking or wax-resist process is simple: It is the application of wax to fabric to prevent (or "resist") dye from coloring specific areas. It's how that wax is added to the fabric surface that makes the difference in the final look of the fabric.

The following pages will introduce you to a variety of batik patterning tools and their uses. Some, like the tjanting tool and tjap—or chop, as it's also called—are unique to wax resist and may be purchased through local craft stores or online. Others are created from everyday items that are as close as your grocery store. All make for enjoyable and creative experimentation.

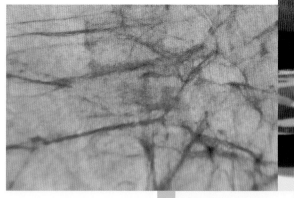

By adjusting the ratio of paraffin to beeswax, you can control the amount of "crackle" in your fabric.

Working with Wax Resist

In order to pattern your fabric with wax, you'll need to prepare the wax and ready the fabric.

Perhaps the first question that comes to mind is, "What kind of wax are we referring to here? Paraffin? Beeswax?" The answer is a combination of waxes, and that mix depends on personal preference. Because each has distinct qualities, you need both paraffin and beeswax to create wax suitable for the batiking process. Beeswax strengthens the wax mixture; paraffin is essential to ensure a smooth flow of wax and creates batik's unique crackle. My personal preference is a 50/50 mixture, though if you prefer more crackle, then you might experiment with a 75 percent paraffin/25 percent beeswax combination. It's important to keep a balance, though, because too much beeswax yields a wax that doesn't flow, and an excess of paraffin creates a wax that breaks apart on the surface of the fabric.

There are a couple of ways to get the desired mixture. One option is to purchase a pre-mixed combination of beeswax and paraffin. Most dye supply houses sell this combination identified as a "batik wax" mix. These pre-mixed combinations tend to be pretty high in paraffin as compared to beeswax. The reason for this is pure economics. Beeswax is substantially more expensive than paraffin. I'm not a huge fan of these pre-fabricated batik waxes, but they are very convenient if mixing your own is not your cup of tea.

My much-preferred method is to mix the wax myself based on weight. Beeswax is readily available in one-pound (453.6 g) blocks at local craft stores. Melt the pound of beeswax with a one-pound (453.6 g) block of paraffin, available with the canning supplies at your local grocery store, and you have a half-and-half combination. This method works equally well if you prefer a different ratio. Use a kitchen scale to weigh the different waxes, and then melt them together to create your desired combination.

Melting the Wax

If the thought of melting wax has given you the impression that this is a stovetop process, banish that thought immediately. For many years I did this step in my backyard under a covered porch. Nowadays, I do all my waxing and dyeing in a studio located in my garage. Working with wax is fun, easy, affordable, creative, and exciting. It is not, however, an indoor process.

The best and safest way to melt wax is using a temperature-controlled electric frying pan in a well-ventilated place. (Don't even think about using a pan and a hot plate.) The frying pan doesn't need to be brand new, but it should have a working temperature gauge. Also, once you've consigned the electric frying pan to melting wax, do not attempt to reclaim it for cooking.

My experience has been that wax heated to 225 degrees Fahrenheit (107.2 degrees Celsius) flows well and is not at risk of smoking. (It will melt at a lower temperature but won't be hot enough to flow.) With an electric frying pan, there's no guesswork regarding the temperature.

I usually melt one pound (453.6 g) of beeswax with one pound (453.6 g) of paraffin. When I'm finished patterning, I can let any excess wax cool in the frying pan and store it to use for my next patterning session.

Supplies

- Beeswax
- Paraffin
- Pre-combined batik wax (if you've decided not to mix your own)
- Temperature-controlled electric frying pan
- Worktable with protective covering

The Melting Process

1. Add beeswax and paraffin or pre-combined mix to electric frying pan.

2. Adjust temperature to 225 degrees Fahrenheit (107.2 degrees Celsius). Maintain this temperature throughout the process.

3. Allow wax to melt completely. (I usually give it about 15 minutes, enough time for wax to become liquid.) When wax is completely melted, you are ready to prepare the fabric for patterning.

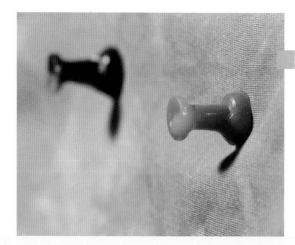

Use tacks or pushpins to secure stretched fabric over box opening.

Preparing and Patterning Fabric

The kind of cotton fabric you use matters. For the best results with the wax-resist methods described in this book, select a quality pima or Egyptian cotton; that is, one with a thread count of at least 130 × 70 threads per inch (2.5 cm). You can purchase this fine fabric from the supplier of your dyes or at the fabric store.

Do not use muslin or Kona cotton for batik. These fabrics are fine for simple dyeing, but have too low a thread count for wax resist; you may find that you are not able to remove the wax even after repeated attempts to boil it out. The same is true for adding wax to already printed commercial cottons. The wax goes in, but it doesn't always come out.

Always pre-wash your fabric before you begin the wax-resist process. This is true even if the fabric claims it is PFD (Prepared For Dye). You don't need to purchase a special detergent. Whatever you normally use is fine. Once washed, your fabric can be dried on a clothesline or in the dryer.

Supplies

Items with an asterisk will be referred to as "wax set-up supplies" in future Supplies lists.

- Apron to protect clothing
- Large cardboard box with top removed or folded in to use as stretching frame*
- Melted wax*
- Patterning tools (brushes, stamps, found objects, etc.)
- Pima cotton fabric with high thread count: ½ yard (0.46 m) to 1 yard (0.91 m)*
- Scrap cardboard to catch drips
- Tacks or pushpins*

Basic Patterning Technique

Depending on the design I'm planning, I usually start my patterning in the center of the fabric.

1. Center and stretch cotton fabric taut across open end of cardboard box.

2. Secure fabric along outside of box with tacks or pushpins.

Reposition fabric to continue patterning.

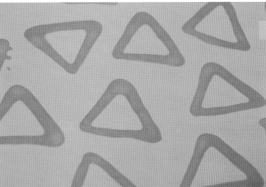

Patterned fabric before overdyeing

The same fabric after overdyeing

3. Heat patterning tool in wax for a few minutes before initial use. *Note:* It's important that the wax runs clear when used. If the wax becomes opaque, re-dip the patterning tool in the wax.

4. Holding a scrap of cardboard beneath the tool to catch dripping wax, apply wax to fabric using patterning tool. Re-dip tool in wax before each application.

5. When stretched fabric surface is patterned as desired, remove tacks, remove fabric from cardboard frame, and reposition to pattern other areas.

6. Continue to pattern, reposition, and secure fabric until entire fabric is patterned as desired.

7. When you are finished applying tool as desired, proceed to dye (or overdye) patterned fabric. (See Basic Dyeing Technique, page 49.)

TAKE NOTE

Do not move the wax pot when the wax is melted (and still hot). Always wait until the wax has cooled and hardened before storing it.

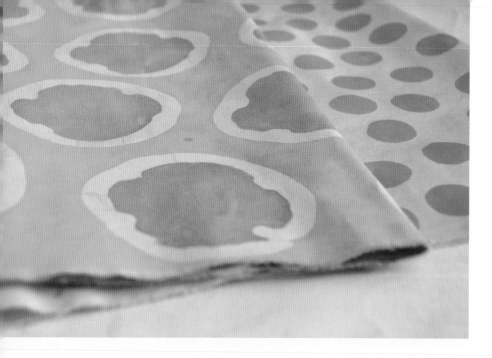

Technique One: Stamping with Found Objects

In setting up your waxing and dyeing space, you've already learned that many of the necessary materials can be found at your local supermarket. Well, many of the tools you'll use to stamp and pattern fabric can be found there, too. Whether you search the produce bins or the shelves of paper goods, you'll soon discover the grocery store is rife with stamping materials.

Consider for a moment the lowly potato. Many of us have memories of making potato stamps in kindergarten. If only we'd known then that this crafty and tasty tool could produce wonderful patterns when dipped in wax and applied to fabric.

Before you exit the produce section, don't forget to add celery, carrots, and bell peppers to your cart. All these veggies make fun, simple, and graphic patterns on fabric. And, best of all, once you're done stamping with them, you can just discard or, better yet, compost your used tool.

Cardboard inserts, from paper-towel to wrapping-paper rolls, also make great patterning tools; for example, you can use them to pattern a variety of differently sized circles. Cardboard scraps cut from discarded boxes (of which there is an abundant and free supply at most markets) can become the source of an endless variety of patterns, affording you the opportunity to fashion all manner of shapes. (See Cardboard Stamps, page 30.) These simple-to-acquire, easy-to-afford (and often free) materials make some of the best and most flexible patterning tools.

No matter which of these simple stamps you try, you can count on fabrics with crisp, clear, and repeatable images that are perfect for cutting up and piecing into quilts or using as whole cloth in totes or pillows. The images are so versatile that you'll find fabrics patterned with found-object stamps in many of the featured projects, including the *Ovals Pillow Cover* (page 92) and the *Shoo Fly Bed Quilt* (page 115).

There are many similarities in how you craft and use various found-object stamps, but each has some unique characteristics and variations.

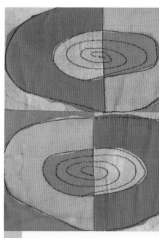

Detail of *Ovals Pillow Cover*

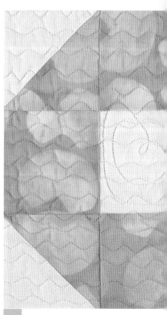

Detail of *Shoo Fly Bed Quilt*

Carved potatoes, ready to be
used as stamps

You can cut a motif
with a cookie
cutter or freehand
with a knife.

Cut a handle in your
stamp for easy use.

Potato Stamps

Once sliced in half, potatoes can be carved to
create a variety of stamps.

Supplies
- Cookie cutters (optional)
- Kitchen or steak knife
- Large, uncooked baking potatoes
- Scrap cardboard for catching drips
- Wax set-up supplies (see page 24)

Creating the Stamp

1. Using a kitchen or steak knife, slice
   potato in half across its width.

2. If using a cookie cutter, impress cutter
   into potato to create shape. Remove
   cookie cutter and use knife to cut away
   potato parts, leaving only those areas
   you want to print.
   OR
   If cutting freehand, use a knife to cut
   away potato parts, leaving only those
   areas you want to print.

3. Create handle for potato stamp
   by cutting away two wedges on the
   uncut end, leaving about ½" (1.3 cm) of
   uncut potato.

Fabric made with a potato stamp

Patterning

Refer to Melting the Wax (page 23) and Preparing and Patterning Fabric (page 24) as needed.

1. Stretch fabric taut over cardboard frame and tack in place along outside edges.

2. Dip carved end of potato in wax until heated. It will take a few minutes for the potato to heat up. The potato *must* be warm for it to function as an effective stamp.

3. Apply stamp to fabric. Refer to Stamp Placement (at right) for patterning ideas.

4. Repeat steps 2 and 3 until stretched area of fabric is patterned as desired.

5. Once stretched fabric surface is completely stamped, remove fabric from frame and reposition to stamp other areas.

6. When finished applying stamps as desired, proceed to dye stamped fabric. (See Basic Dyeing Technique, page 49.)

The image is stamped in rows parallel to the top or side edge of fabric.

The image is stamped randomly; that is, without a set pattern.

The image is stamped in staggered bands.

Stamp Placement

After you've carved, crafted, or found the perfect stamp, you need to consider its placement on your fabric. At left are three possibilities for creating patterns with stamps.

Apply stamping tools by pressing them firmly onto the stretched fabric and, once the fabric is stamped, lifting the tool straight up from the fabric surface. It isn't necessary to rock the tool back and forth on the fabric surface. If you can't fit a full repeat of the stamped image on the stretched surface of the fabric, wait until you've repositioned the fabric to stamp again.

Fabric made with a carrot stamp

Veggie Stamps

The produce section of the grocery store provides a bountiful harvest of stamping materials. The best vegetables for making stamps are those that have a naturally low water content, such as carrots, celery, and bell peppers.

Supplies

- Kitchen knife
- Scrap cardboard for catching drips
- Vegetables such as carrots, celery, and bell peppers
- Wax set-up supplies (see page 24)

Creating the Stamp

Cut off about one-third of the carrot or celery; discard. Cut bell pepper in half, discard half without stem, and remove seeds.

These veggies are ready to be used as stamps. Like the potato, all veggies must be warm to function effectively.

Patterning

Refer to Melting the Wax (page 23) and Preparing and Patterning Fabric (page 24) as needed.

1. Stretch fabric taut over cardboard frame and tack in place along outside edges.

2. Holding carrot or celery by remaining length or holding pepper by its stem, dip cut edge of vegetable in wax until heated.

3. Apply stamp to fabric. Refer to Stamp Placement (page 28) for patterning ideas.

4. Repeat steps 2 and 3 until stretched area of fabric is patterned as desired.

5. Once stretched fabric surface is completely stamped, remove fabric from frame and reposition to stamp other areas.

6. When finished applying stamps as desired, proceed to dye stamped fabric. (See Basic Dyeing Technique, page 49.)

Cardboard stamps are versatile, accessible, and easy to use.

Cardboard Stamps

These may be the simplest of stamps, but that doesn't stop them from having a powerful impact. Use pre-formed shapes, such as cardboard tubes from paper towels, or create your own in a variety of geometric motifs.

Supplies

You will need the items with an asterisk only if you plan to make your own cardboard stamps.

- Cardboard scraps, at least 12" × 3" (30.5 cm × 7.6 cm)*
- Cardboard tubes
- Pencil*
- Postal tape*
- Quilter's clear ruler*
- Scrap cardboard for catching drips
- Self-healing cutting mat*
- Utility knife*
- Wax set-up supplies (see page 24)

Creating Stamps

The possibilities are almost endless, but to get you started, I'm including instructions for three options. Consider making similar shapes in different sizes to stamp nesting shapes, or combining shapes to make a new image. *Note:* The given sizes of the various shapes are just examples. Adjust measurements to craft the size desired.

Square Stamps

1. Using utility knife and quilter's ruler, cut cardboard into strip measuring 12" × 3" (30.5 cm × 7.6 cm).

2. Measure 3" (7.6 cm) segments along long edge and mark with pencil.

3. Score lines along marks with ruler and utility knife.

4. Fold cardboard along scored lines to form a square.

5. Using postal tape, tape short edges together to secure square.

Score lines along marks.

Tape short edges to form square.

Fabrics made with cardboard stamps

Triangle Stamps

1. Using utility knife and quilter's ruler, cut cardboard into strip measuring 12" × 3" (30.5 cm × 7.6 cm).

2. Measure 4" (10.2 cm) segments along long edge and mark with pencil.

3. Score lines along marks with ruler and utility knife.

4. Fold cardboard along scored lines to form a triangle.

5. Using postal tape, tape short edges together to secure triangle.

Nesting Stamps

1. Using utility knife and quilter's ruler, cut one cardboard rectangle in each of following sizes: 12" × 3" (30.5 cm × 7.6 cm), 9" × 3" (22.9 cm × 7.6 cm), 6" × 3" (15.2 cm × 7.6 cm), and 3" × 3" (7.6 cm × 7.6 cm).

2. Measure to find midpoint along long edge of each cardboard piece and mark with pencil.

3. Score a line along mark on each cardboard piece with ruler and utility knife.

4. Fold each cardboard piece along scored line.

Patterning

Refer to Melting the Wax (page 23) and Preparing and Patterning Fabric (page 24) as needed.

1. Stretch fabric taut over cardboard frame and tack in place along outside edges.

2. Dip cardboard stamp into wax until heated.

3. Apply stamp to fabric. Refer to Stamp Placement (page 28) for patterning ideas.

4. Repeat steps 2 and 3 until stretched area of fabric is patterned as desired.

5. Once stretched fabric surface is completely stamped, remove fabric from frame and reposition to stamp other areas.

6. When finished applying stamps as desired, proceed to dye stamped fabric. (See Basic Dyeing Technique, page 49.)

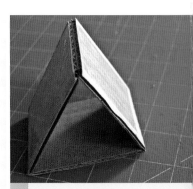

Tape short edges to form triangle.

Folded, finished nesting stamps

TAKE NOTE

You can stamp folded pieces as nesting shapes or print them individually.

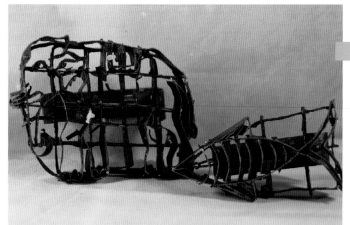

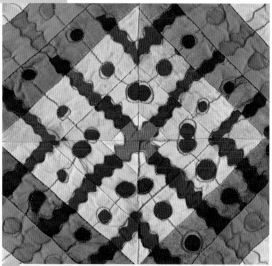

A pair of traditional metal tjaps

Technique Two: Using Traditional Wax-Resist Tools

While batik may not be as old as time, it has been around for a long while and has several traditional patterning tools, including the tjanting tool and the wooden and metal block, also known as a tjap or chop. Although these tools constitute the "old guard" of batik methods, they can still read as remarkably fresh and modern.

As is the case for fabrics made with many techniques in this book, fabrics patterned with traditional tools can work in a variety of projects. Both tjanting tools and wooden or metal blocks can create fabric with smaller patterns ideal for cutting up and using in quilts, totes, coasters, pillows, and garments. These fabrics can be used exclusively or in combination with fabrics patterned using other techniques. For instance, in the *E Block Quilt* (page 120), all the fabric was stamped using one wooden block, while in the *Shoo Fly Bed Quilt* (page 115), fabrics crafted with tjanting tools and wooden blocks are pieced alongside fabrics created with other techniques.

Detail of *E Block Quilt*

Detail of *Shoo Fly Bed Quilt*

Traditional tjanting tool

Tjanting Tool

Probably the best-known traditional wax-resist tool is the tjanting tool, an all-in-one spout and metal pot attached to a wooden handle. The pot keeps the wax hot as it pours from the fine-pointed spout; the wooden handle protects the user from the heat of the metal.

If I could name only one reason why you should add a tjanting tool to your batik tool kit, it would be line quality. No brush or stamp can lay wax down on fabric quite the way a tjanting tool does. Consider it this way: A tjanting tool is to batik what a fountain pen is to calligraphy. Since the wax is kept hot, and the spout is curved to allow the quick flow of wax, the resulting mark is amazingly fluid. Combine that flowing line with a simple, repeated motif such as a swirl or circle and you have some beautifully patterned fabric.

The tjanting tool takes a bit of getting used to, but with a little practice, you'll soon be drawing lines as fluid as the wax that flows from the spout of this unique "pen."

Another selling point for the tjanting tool is variety. There are choices in terms of single- or double-spouted tools, as well as different spout widths. My best advice is to invest in a few options and see which one(s) you like best. You may discover that the tjanting tool you prefer differs depending upon the type of patterning or project.

Supplies

- Scrap cardboard for catching drips
- Tjanting tool
- Wax set-up supplies (see page 24)

Fabrics made with
a tjanting tool

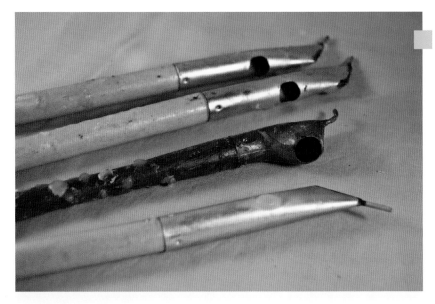

Tjanting tools come in a variety of spout widths, as well as in single- and double-spouted versions.

Patterning

Refer to Melting the Wax (page 23) and Preparing and Patterning Fabric (page 24) as needed. Because the wax tends to flow quickly, it's a good idea to experiment with patterning and controlling the tool before applying wax to your fabric. You can do this on a scrap of muslin stretched across your cardboard-box frame or even on a plain piece of paper.

1. Stretch fabric taut over cardboard frame and tack in place along outside edges.

2. Dip tjanting tool in wax, making sure that attached metal pot is fully immersed.

3. Holding cardboard scrap underneath tool to catch drips, transfer tjanting tool to fabric. Working quickly, make markings on fabric as desired until wax no longer runs clear.

4. Return tjanting tool to wax pot. Reheat tool and repeat step 3 until stretched area of fabric is patterned as desired.

5. Once stretched fabric surface is completely patterned, remove fabric from frame and reposition to other areas.

6. When finished applying tool as desired, proceed to dye patterned fabric. (See Basic Dyeing Technique, page 49.)

Use a cardboard scrap to catch drips when transferring tool to fabric.

Wooden and copper blocks come in a variety of designs.

Wooden or Metal Blocks

In addition to the tjanting tool, there are also wooden and copper blocks specific to wax resist. These traditional tools can yield the type of imagery we typically associate with batik: patterns that are intricate, densely packed, abstracted shapes. However, they are equally useful in creating more contemporary-looking patterning.

In much the same way that tjanting tools yield results that cannot be achieved through other means, traditionally carved wooden blocks or metal blocks fashioned from copper create patterning that is distinct from other methods of wax stamping. The back of each block features a large handle, which makes the block easier to manipulate. Both wooden and copper blocks are crafted so that the wax adheres only to the surface image, ensuring a crisp print. In the case of the copper block, the heat-conducting metal allows the wax to remain hot longer.

The imagery commonly seen on these blocks ranges from geometric to flowers to animals. My personal preference is for simple, geometric designs. These seem to print best, and the bold, uncluttered images are a little more forgiving to work with.

Of course, working with these blocks means working with a predetermined image. What amazes me, though, are the new images that emerge when these stamps are applied randomly or in rows.

Supplies

- Scrap cardboard for catching drips
- Stamps: copper and/or wooden
- Wax set-up supplies (see page 24)

TAKE NOTE

Since the primary function of these stamps is to create repeat patterns, registration of the stamp is important. I find it helps to start patterning in the center of fabric. To find the center, fold and crease fabric lengthwise, open, refold, and re-crease the fabric widthwise.

The traditional block shown at right was used to pattern these colorful fabrics.

Patterning

Refer to Melting the Wax (page 23) and Preparing and Patterning Fabric (page 24) as needed.

1. Stretch fabric taut over cardboard frame and tack in place along outside edges.

2. Hold stamp by handle and dip in wax until stamp is heated. Allow stamp to heat thoroughly.

3. Apply stamp to fabric. Refer to Stamp Placement (page 28) for patterning ideas.

4. Repeat steps 2 and 3 until stretched area of fabric is patterned as desired.

5. Once stretched fabric surface is completely stamped, remove fabric from frame and reposition to stamp other areas.

6. When finished applying stamps as desired, proceed to dye stamped fabric. (See Basic Dyeing Technique, page 49.)

A simple wine cork can transform a letterpress stamp into a useful batiking tool.

Converting Letterpress Stamps to Batik Tools

I have quite a few letterpress stamps, and until recently I wasn't quite sure why I was collecting them. Then it dawned on me that all these stamps needed to become ideal for batik were handles.

Enter my other quirky collection: wine corks. Pair these two items, secure with glue, and a stamp is born.

Supplies

- Letterpress stamps, at least 2" (5.1 cm) tall
- Wine corks
- Wood glue or other strong glue

Making the Stamp

1. Depending on the size of your letterpress stamp, glue 1–3 corks to the back of block.

2. Allow 24 hours for glue to dry.

Fabric patterned with a converted letterpress stamp, and the stamp used to pattern it

Technique Three:
Patterning with Brushes

As a rule, I try to avoid painting anything with too broad a brush, unless what I'm painting is fabric and my brush is loaded with melted wax. Then, no matter the width of my brush, I've got a simple batik tool that's capable of creating a multiplicity of patterns and images.

As tools go, they don't get much more basic than a brush, but it's important not to discount the beauty of marks made with this simple implement. Brushes come in so many sizes, shapes, and widths that they are really a whole category of tools. My personal favorites are calligraphy brushes and wide workhorses more commonly associated with house painting, but there are an amazing plethora of brushes made from a variety of fibers, both natural and synthetic, so your choices are pretty extensive.

However, before you dip your beloved sable brush into the wax pot, you should be aware of one fact. Once you've used a brush for wax, it is for all eternity a wax brush.

From delicate calligraphy brushes to hefty house-paint varieties, different brushes make different markings.

You never will be able to remove the wax completely, and therefore the brush only will function as a soft, supple tool capable of making fluid marks when it is loaded with hot, melted wax.

Does this mean that you should consign only cheap, semi-disposable brushes to use with wax? Absolutely not. Quality tools are essential. Just don't expect this particular tool to multitask.

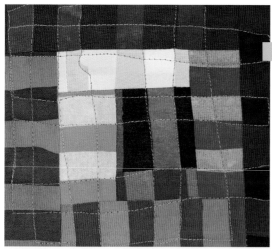

One of four *Stripey Stripped Coasters*

Versatility of Design

Versatility of design is probably the biggest plus of working with brushes. When you use stamps, you can vary the placement and density of your stamped image, but there's not much possibility that your cardboard circle won't read as a circle. This is not true with a brush, where your imagination dictates the image. If you want lines, you can draw lines. If you want trees, you can draw trees. If you want a portrait of your cat, nothing but good taste stands in your way. My personal aesthetic and experience leans toward abstract patterning rather than realistic depiction, but it's important to know that—with the right brush—the possibilities for images are almost limitless.

Since the types of images possible are so varied, the uses for the fabric made using this tool are wide-ranging. You can use this technique to create fabric used as whole cloth, to be embellished, or as material destined to be cut and pieced for patchwork.

In this book, projects such as the *Stripey Stripped Coasters* (page 66) and *What's on Top Mini-Quilt* (page 97) highlight the beauty of lines made with brushes.

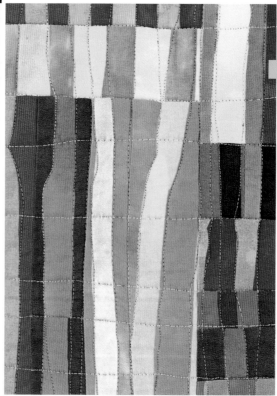

Detail of *What's on Top Mini-Quilt*

Fabrics made by applying wax with brushes

Applying the Wax

Regardless of the final image, the process for applying wax with a brush is like the tool itself: simple.

Supplies

- Brushes, variety of sizes
- Scrap cardboard for catching drips
- Wax set-up supplies (see page 24)

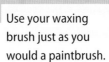

Use your waxing brush just as you would a paintbrush.

Patterning

Refer to Melting the Wax (page 23) and Preparing and Patterning Fabric (page 24) as needed. You might want to keep an inspirational sketch or photo of a particular pattern or image nearby to refer to as you work.

1. Stretch fabric taut over cardboard frame and tack in place along outside edges.

2. Dip brush in wax, allowing a few minutes for brush to heat thoroughly.

3. Using brush, apply wax to fabric.

4. Repeat steps 2 and 3 until stretched area of fabric is patterned as desired.

5. Once stretched fabric surface is completely patterned, remove fabric from frame and reposition to pattern other areas.

6. When finished patterning as desired, proceed to dye patterned fabric. (See Basic Dyeing Technique, page 49.)

TAKE NOTE

Allow your brushes to cool before storing them bristles side up in a jar or other similar container. There is no need to clean the brushes; the wax simply hardens and will be reheated the next time you use them.

Layering

Working with wax resist can yield beautiful fabric with very little effort. Many of my favorite fabrics are created by patterning with wax on white fabric and overdyeing in a single color. One of the joys of this method, though, is not being limited to one color or even one way of achieving a second, third, or fourth layer of color and pattern.

There are basically two ways to create multi-hued fabric without relying on other processes such as discharging. The first is called *additive*, and the name is pretty self-descriptive. Wax is applied to fabric and the fabric is dyed. (See Basic Dyeing Technique, page 49.) Then the fabric is removed from the dye bath, rinsed, allowed to dry, and more wax is applied. The fabric is immersed in a second dye bath, usually of a darker color. At that point, the process can be repeated or the fabric can be finished according to the instructions in Finishing Up: Aftercare for Waxed and Dyed Fabric (page 54). What makes this method additive is that wax is added after each dye immersion and not removed until all the color has been applied.

After one layer of waxing, the fabric is patterned with stripes in two colors. A second row of waxed stripes and an additional dye bath creates a more complex fabric.

42

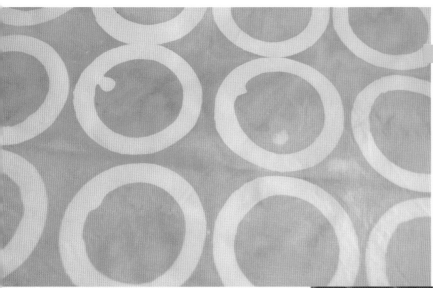

Wax is removed after the first dye bath to allow for more patterning.

An alternative method for layering wax and color is to remove the wax after each dye immersion. In this case, begin with an unwaxed length of fabric. After adding some patterning with wax, and soaking the fabric in a dye bath, remove the wax according to the process described in Finishing Up: Aftercare for Waxed and Dyed Fabric (page 54). At this point, the fabric is completely "open," meaning that it is free from any wax resist. Rather than calling it done, add new wax patterning and then dye the fabric a second time. You might then decide that the piece is complete and remove the wax as a final step, or you might repeat the wax removal/re-patterning/overdyeing process. At some point, of course, you'll need to complete the fabric by removing the wax and washing it based on the instructions in Finishing Up: Aftercare for Waxed and Dyed Fabric.

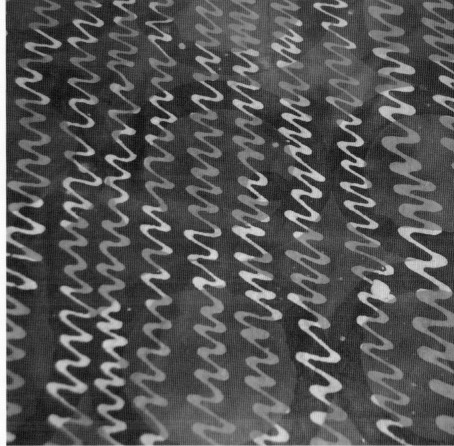

Interest is created with both additional coloring and by combining different patterning techniques.

Note the differences in color between the discharged areas and the areas that were protected by the wax.

Technique Four: Discharging and Overdyeing

One of the reasons I was drawn to printmaking early in my artistic career was the seemingly endless ways I could combine a few techniques to create a multiplicity of effects. Images could be drawn, chemically erased, redrawn, and layered. When I began to explore working with wax, it was discharging and overdyeing that most reminded me of these techniques. I loved the idea that marks previously made could be "erased," while other areas could be waxed and overdyed. The combination of discharging and overdyeing allows for the creation of color and pattern mixes not possible with the standard "wax then dye" technique.

Discharging is really just a fancy way of saying bleaching or removing color. Most discharging is done with diluted household bleach, although there are specific chemicals available through dye suppliers for color removal. These color-removal chemicals do as they advertise, but I personally prefer bleach because it is inexpensive and readily available.

What Discharging Will— and Won't—Do

It is important to note that discharging a previously dyed fabric will not bleach that fabric back to white. The resulting shade of a discharged fabric is heavily dependent on the color the fabric was dyed originally. However, when discharging is done properly, there should be a marked difference between the fabric that was protected by wax and the fabric that was discharged. Red fabric will discharge to a pale pink, brown to ecru, and some colors—such as turquoise—will get close to the original white.

44

Discharging can be an end in itself. You might dye a length of fabric chocolate brown, apply wax using one of the previously described patterning techniques, discharge the unwaxed areas, and call it a day. However, I feel you could be missing out on one of the biggest advantages of coupling bleaching with wax resist. Because of the transparency of the dyes used, color mixing is an inevitable result of multiple dye baths. For instance, fabric dyed yellow, then patterned with wax, will—when immersed in a red dye bath—yield orange. The result will be a yellow pattern on an orange background. The only way that I know to get around this scenario is through discharging. You still begin with the same yellow fabric and apply the same pattern. But before you dye the fabric red, you discharge that fabric and get it as close to white as possible. When you then immerse the fabric in the red dye bath, you will get a much truer red than had you layered that color over yellow.

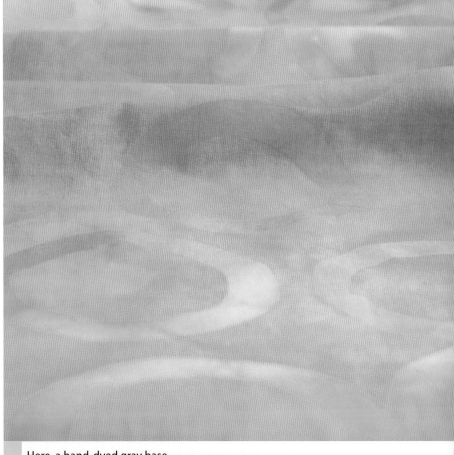

Here, a hand-dyed gray base fabric was discharged and then immersed in a yellow dye bath; otherwise, the overlaid yellow would have created a green background color.

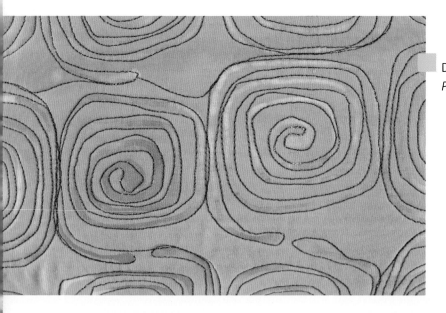

Detail of *Show-Off Pillow Cover*

Consider the fabric I created for the *Show-Off Pillow Cover* (page 88). The original, unwaxed fabric was dyed gray. The swirly shapes were applied in wax using a tjanting tool, and then the entire piece was discharged. Once I was satisfied with how much color was removed, I overdyed the fabric in a golden yellow.

If I had started with white fabric, dyed it yellow, waxed the swirls, and then overdyed the fabric gray, I would have had yellow swirls on a greenish-gray background. The original yellow would be altered by the gray to create a new color. This may turn out to be quite lovely, but it was not my original intent.

Another reason to try discharging is the ability to get three layers of patterning and color from two dye-bath immersions. Returning to our example of using a yellow base fabric, you can pattern the fabric with wax, discharge the unwaxed areas, and then add more wax patterning before immersing the fabric in red. You then get three colors and two opportunities to add patterning with just two dye applications. How's that for getting more bang for your dyeing buck?

But wait, there's more. How about patterning the fabric with wax, dyeing that fabric, removing the wax, adding new wax patterning, and then discharging and overdyeing? Are you getting the picture? The possibilities for experimentation are limited only by your imagination, yet the recipe for discharging is simple to prepare and use.

It took just two dye baths to get this multi-hued fabric.

Stopping the Bleach

An important consideration when working with bleach is how to *stop* the bleaching action. Here, too, you've got a couple of choices in product.

My bleach-stop method involves the use of diluted vinegar. I have been using this method for at least 15 years and have been very pleased with the results. There are those who contend that this method doesn't work, that it harms the fabric, and that it creates noxious fumes. This has not been my experience. When I discharge fabric, I always do so in a well-ventilated place. The vinegar solution I use is heavily diluted with water, and I *always* wash my fabrics in the washing machine with detergent as part of my finishing process. Additionally, I use the vinegar bath partly as a bleach stop, but primarily because I have observed that moving fabric back and forth between the bleach and water bath and the diluted vinegar bath removes more color than bleach alone.

There are a number of commercial products you can substitute if you prefer an alternative to my vinegar-bath method. These chemicals, available through dye suppliers, can be mixed with water and used as a final rinse to stop the action of bleach. Nevertheless, my preference is diluted vinegar.

By now you've probably figured out that the potential of patterning, discharging, and overdyeing is practically endless.

Discharging with Bleach

This simple process truly is a gateway to creating complex patterning. Think of it as your "eraser" for fabric; it allows you to make room for more imagery and to control the juxtaposition of colors.

Supplies

- Cotton fabric*
- Dishwashing gloves
- Dust mask or respirator
- Household bleach
- Measuring cup**
- One-gallon (3.8 liters) calibrated bucket or pitcher
- Tongs**
- Two standard-sized dishpans
- Vinegar or commercial bleach-stop product
- Water

Fabric can be waxed and dyed in a single shade or waxed and dyed several times. The key is to have some color already on the fabric.

**Do not reuse these items for cooking.*

The Discharge Process

Work in a well-ventilated place, preferably outside or in a garage with the door open.

Wear gloves to protect your hands and a dust mask or respirator. If you are using a commercial bleach-stop product, mix according to package directions and substitute for vinegar in the following steps.

1. Pour 2½ quarts (2.4 liters) of water into each dishpan.

2. Mix 1 cup (0.2 liter) of bleach into one dishpan.

3. Mix 1 cup (0.2 liter) of vinegar into second dishpan.

4. Place fabric in bleach solution and allow to sit for a few minutes.

5. Using tongs, transfer fabric to vinegar bath and allow to sit for a few minutes.

6. Continue moving fabric between bleach and vinegar baths until unwaxed areas of fabric cease to lighten. Finish with fabric in vinegar bath.

7. If you are planning to overdye fabric, refer to Basic Dyeing Technique (page 49). If you are not planning to overdye fabric, rinse thoroughly with water, and refer to Finishing Up: Aftercare for Waxed and Dyed Fabric (page 54) for instructions regarding wax removal.

Basic Dyeing Technique

Until several years ago, I'd never baked a loaf of bread. Actually, I didn't bake anything that involved yeast. I thought it was too complicated. I worried that it wouldn't proof properly or that my dough wouldn't rise. I worried that I would be a bread-baking failure. But then one day I ran across a simple, easy-to-follow recipe and I realized that it wasn't that difficult after all.

Why tell you this story? Because if concern about being a fabric-dyeing failure has stopped you in the past, I'm here to provide you with the easy-to-follow recipe that will simplify the process and allay your fears. And, if plain lack of knowledge has stopped you, this same recipe will remedy that, too.

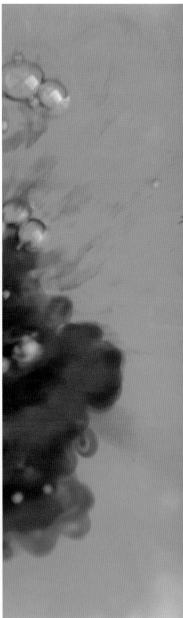

The only "specialty" item you need for dyeing fabric is the dye.

A Forgiving Process

To bring the baking analogy full circle, I suppose I should note that dyeing is actually more like cooking than baking. Whereas baking requires exact measurements, cooking is a little more forgiving, and absolute amounts are often replaced with a pinch of this or a dash of that. This is true of dyeing as well.

This chapter includes a table (page 53) with specific "ingredient" amounts that will yield a color very close to the one pictured in the swatches available from the dye supplier. However, once you get comfortable with the process, you might consider varying the amount of dye you add to the mix to see what value of the desired color you can achieve. Having learned most of this process through my own experimentation, I find that I'm a big proponent of just seeing what happens.

In addition to the process being simple, the necessary materials are, with one possible exception, easily accessible. The grocery store is a primary source. Among the ingredients you'll find there are salt, water softener, measuring tools, and a dishpan. Soda ash—the chemical that activates the dye bath—can be purchased at a pool supply store for substantially less than from a dye supplier. The star of the show, the fabric, is available at your local fabric store.

The only item you may need to purchase online is the dye itself. You may be able to find fiber-reactive, cold-water dyes (along with color swatches) at your local craft store. If not, do an Internet search for them; you'll find dye suppliers and color swatches online. The table on page 53 should produce a color that is similar to the manufacturer's color swatches, whether you purchase the dyes locally or buy them online.

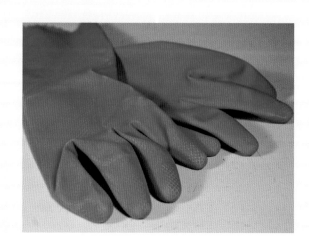

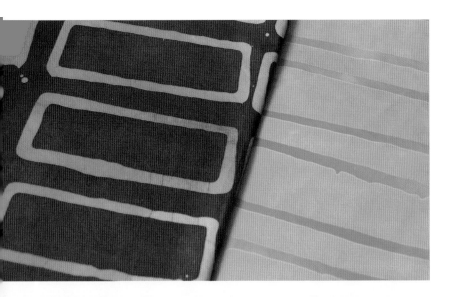

Safety First

Before we get to the measuring and mixing, it's important to discuss a few safety guidelines. These dyes can be allergenic in powder form, so protect yourself by taking the following simple precautions.

First, never, *ever*, no matter how much you might need that measuring tablespoon to add just the right amount of salt to your stroganoff, use dye tools in the kitchen. Once a measuring cup or spoon has been used for or even around dye, do not return it to kitchen use. It's best to purchase these items with the specific intention of reserving them for use with dyes.

Next, always work in a well-ventilated place, and wear rubber gloves and a respirator or dust mask when measuring and handling dyes.

Finally, do not eat or drink while working with dyes. Dye powder is very fine and if you bring food or beverages into your dye space, you may inadvertently ingest some of that powder. While this won't make you sick, it also isn't good for you. So schedule your snack either before or after your dye session. Make working safely a habit, so you can focus more freely on patterning and color creation.

The Dyeing Process

The recipe is simple and the materials easy to obtain, but the quality of color you'll get when you dye your own fabric is truly unique.

Supplies

Refer to chart on page 53 for exact amounts of items marked with an asterisk.

- Cotton fabric*
- Dishpan
- Fiber-reactive, cold-water dye powder in your choice of color*
- Measuring cup
- Measuring spoons
- One gallon (3.8 liters) calibrated bucket or pitcher
- Respirator or dust mask
- Rubber gloves
- Salt*
- Soda ash*
- Two plastic containers, e.g. empty take-out food or margarine containers
- Water*
- Water softener*

Preparing the Dye Bath

1. Based on amounts listed in the chart on page 53, fill calibrated bucket or pitcher with the appropriate amount of cold tap water.

2. Pour water from bucket into dishpan.

3. Measure and pour salt into dishpan.

4. Measure and add water softener to dishpan.

5. Measure and pour one cup (250 ml) of hot tap water into each plastic container. Hot water is strictly for dissolving dyes and chemicals and amount will not vary.

6. Put on gloves and mask to measure dye powder.

7. Add measured dye powder to water in one plastic container. Mix thoroughly with measuring spoon.

8. Add dissolved dye to dishpan. At this point, you can remove mask.

9. Place fabric in dishpan.

10. Measure soda ash into second plastic container. Mix thoroughly.

11. Add soda ash to dishpan. *Note:* Depending on the dye color, the soda ash may appear to cause a slight color change in the mixture. The final color of the fabric, however, will be similar to the swatches pictured on the dye house website.

Dyeing the Fabric

1. Immerse fabric in dye bath.

2. Allow fabric to soak in dye bath at least 6–8 hours. Move fabric around in bath periodically to ensure good coverage.

3. Remove fabric from dye bath and empty dye bath liquid into sink. In its liquid form, dye is considered non-toxic.

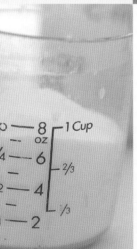

Chemicals and Water	Fabric Amounts		
	½ yard (.46 m)	1 yard (.91 m)	2 yards (1.83 m)
Water	2½ quarts (2.4 liters)	1 gallon (3.8 liters)	1½ gallons (5.7 liters)
Salt	½ cup (125 ml)	1 cup (250 ml)	1½ cups (375 ml)
Water softener	1 tablespoon (15 ml)	1 tablespoon (15 ml)	1 tablespoon (15 ml)
Cold-water dye powder	1 level tablespoon (15 ml)	1 heaping tablespoon (15 ml)	1½ tablespoons (22.5 ml)
Soda ash	4 heaping tablespoons (60 ml)	6 heaping tablespoons (90 ml)	8 heaping tablespoons (120 ml)

54

Chapter 5

Finishing Up: Aftercare for Waxed and Dyed Fabric

Remember when you were a kid in school learning a new craft, and as each of your classmates finished, he or she would call out, "I'm done, now what do I do?" Well, this chapter is devoted to answering that question.

First, pat yourself on the back because if you've made it this far, you've tackled a whole new world of techniques. Then get ready to return your fabric to its soft, pliable state.

When to Wash

As a rule, I wash all my fabrics when I'm done coloring and/or patterning them.

Unwaxed, dyed fabrics can go directly into the washing machine and dryer.

If the fabric has wax resist and you're planning to add more wax or layer another color or technique, hang the fabric on a line to dry before proceeding.

If the dye bath is your final process, and your fabric has wax resist from previous patterning, see Removing the Wax (page 56) for information on how to remove the wax before giving it a final wash.

Removing the Wax

I'm sure you've noticed that the wax you used to create patterning on your fabric has also made it rather stiff. Luckily, there's an easy process for removing the wax. All you need is an inexpensive stockpot, some water, and your stovetop to boil out the wax. This, along with a thorough wash in your washing machine, and your fabric is ready to be cut, sewn, quilted, or just admired.

Like removal of the wax, disposal of the water and wax collected during the boil-out process is also a simple matter. Just allow the stockpot to cool to room temperature, dump the contents down the toilet, and flush. Because the water and wax are no longer warm, they won't damage your pipes, and that particular pipe is one of the larger pipes exiting your house. I've been doing this for years and I've yet to clog a toilet.

Folks often ask me if they should wash their batiked fabrics separately to prevent any dye from bleeding onto other fabrics.

My response is to point out that this fabric has been boiled in a pot at 212 degrees Fahrenheit (100 degrees Celsius) and then machine washed and dried. It's weathered more than any fabric you might purchase at a store. In other words, once you've removed the wax and washed your fabric, it is completely ready to use. You'll also find that your hand-dyed fabrics are wonderfully light and colorfast. They truly are a cut above store-bought fabrics.

Stockpots are inexpensive and easy to find at dollar or thrift stores, but don't use this pot for anything other than boiling wax out of fabric.

Supplies

- Large stockpot
- Laundry detergent
- Plastic bucket
- Rubber gloves
- Sink
- Tongs
- Washer and dryer or clothesline
- Water

Gently rub fabric with fingertips to loosen and remove wax.

The "Boiling Out" Process

1. While wearing rubber gloves, empty dye bath into sink and rinse fabric in cold water.

2. Place fabric in stockpot and fill with warm water until fabric is almost covered.

3. Place stockpot on stove and set heat to medium.

4. Once pot has begun to boil, reduce heat to simmer.

5. Allow pot to simmer for 45–60 minutes. Check fabric periodically and give it a gentle stir with tongs.

6. Turn off heat. Using tongs, remove fabric from pot and place in bucket. Carry bucket to sink.

7. Run a slow stream of warm water into bucket. As warm water hits fabric, wax will begin to crack at the surface.

8. Remove gloves so you can feel for any hidden deposits of wax. Work wax off fabric by gently rubbing fabric surface with fingertips. Allow wax bits to accumulate in bucket. *Note:* This process does not require more than one bucket of water. If there is any wax remaining on the fabric surface, it will be removed by the agitation of the washing machine.

9. Place fabric in washing machine, add detergent, and wash on warm setting.

10. When removing fabric from washing machine, check fabric surface for any bits of remaining wax. These can be picked off by hand.

11. Dry fabric in dryer on regular cotton setting or on clothesline.

12. Dispose of bucket water in toilet.

Chapter 6

A Few Sewing How-Tos

The projects in this book are easily tackled with basic sewing skills. There are, however, a few techniques that—while not exclusive to me—might not be familiar to everyone. They are explained here, with the trickiest parts accompanied by diagrams.

Of course, if you already have a preferred method for basting, or making and adding binding, for example, feel free to use your familiar techniques. The key here is to do "whatever works" to give you an efficient and attractive result.

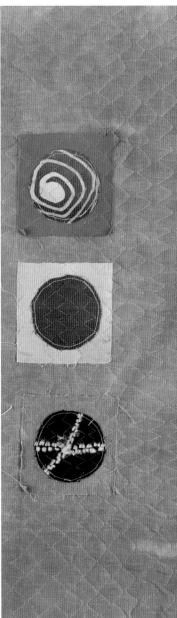

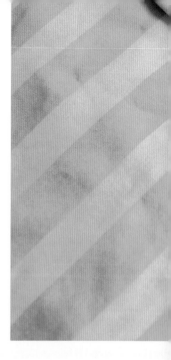

Freehand Rotary Cutting

Several projects in this book call for strips or pieces that are cut freehand to a specific width or size. You can use the technique described here for these projects, as well as for cutting strips for projects that require freehand-cut strips in a variety of widths.

This is an easy technique to master and you'll be amazed at how accurate your eye can be. When you try it the first time or two, you might find it helpful to keep a ruler nearby for visual reference. The more often you use the technique, however, the more accurate you'll become. All you need is a rotary cutter and a self-healing cutting mat.

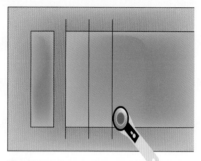

Fig. 1

1. Unfold and place fabric on mat.

2. Using rotary cutter (but no ruler), cut strips of desired width along one fabric edge (Fig. 1). Continue cutting until you have cut desired number of strips.

3. If the project calls for freehand-cut pieces (e.g. *Ovals Pillow Cover*, page 92), you can measure them by eye and cut them from the freehand-cut strips.

Preparing Batting and Backing for Basting

There are a few things to keep in mind when planning your backing and batting for basting.

When determining the size of the batting you will need, the most important factor is whether you will hand or machine quilt the quilt. If you are planning to hand quilt, you will need a batting that is about 10" (25.4 cm) larger than the quilt top in both width and length. This allows you to stretch and secure your quilt sandwich in a hoop.

However, if your finishing plans call for machine quilting, a batting so much larger than the quilt top is neither necessary nor particularly desirable as it creates more bulk to be maneuvered under the head of your sewing machine. An extra 2" (5.1 cm) or so all around is plenty.

The same size standards apply for the backing, and while most projects in this book require a backing that can be accommodated by a single width of fabric—whether you plan to hand or machine

quilt—the *Shoo Fly Bed Quilt* (page 115) requires that you piece the backing in order to make a large enough piece. This is typical practice for a bed-sized quilt.

If, for example, your quilt top is 60" × 80" (152.4 cm × 203.2 cm), you will need about four yards (3.66 m) of fabric for the backing if you plan to machine quilt. Fabric usually comes in 45" (114.3 cm) widths on the bolt, but you will lose some of that width when you launder the fabric and remove the selvages. Therefore, to achieve a backing sufficient for the 60" (152.4 cm) width of the quilt top, divide the fabric in half crosswise (from selvage to selvage), into two 2-yard (1.83 m) pieces. Sew the pieces together along their lengthwise (selvage) edges, and you will create a backing that measures approximately 72" × 84" (182.9 cm × 213.4 cm), which, when turned with the seam running crosswise, is large enough to function as backing for this bed-sized quilt.

Layering and Pin Basting

It has always been my preference to use safety pins for basting. I don't have the patience for thread basting and don't really care for spray basting, so 1" (2.5 cm) safety pins are my basting buddies. The number of pins you'll need will depend upon the size of the top you're basting. Estimate about four pins for every 6" (15.2 cm) square.

1. Place backing fabric, wrong side up, on a clean, firm, flat surface, such as a table-top or floor. Working from the center, carefully smooth out any wrinkles.

2. Secure edges of fabric to work surface with masking tape.

3. Center batting on top of backing and smooth out any wrinkles.

4. Center top, right side up, on backing and batting (Fig. 2). Once again, working from center, smooth out any wrinkles.

5. Starting in center, secure one safety pin through all three layers.

6. Secure a second safety pin approximately hand's distance from first pin. Working in a clockwise direction, continue in this manner until entire quilt sandwich is secured.

7. Remove masking tape, and hand or machine quilt as desired, removing the safety pins as you come to them.

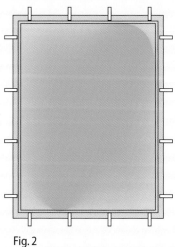

Fig. 2

Fig. 3   Fig. 4

Binding a Quilt or Pillow

This is the binding technique I use for all my quilts and many of my pillows. It is by no means the only way to bind, but I like it for its simplicity.

1. Using diagonal seams, sew together binding strips to create one long strip.

2. Trim batting and backing flush with edges of quilt top.

3. Beginning at the center along one side of the quilt, align raw edge of binding with raw edge of quilt sandwich.

4. Leaving a 4" to 5" (10.2 cm to 12.7 cm) tail of binding strip free, machine stitch binding to quilt sandwich using a ¼" (0.6 cm) seam. Stop sewing ¼" (0.6 cm) from first corner (Fig. 3).

5. Pull sandwich and binding slightly away from machine. Pinch triangle of binding and align along stitched edge. Turn sandwich and binding 90 degrees so that newly mitered corner of binding and next side of quilt sandwich edge fall under right edge of machine foot. Starting at edge of sandwich, resume sewing binding to sandwich with ¼" (0.6 cm) seam (Fig. 4), mitering each corner.

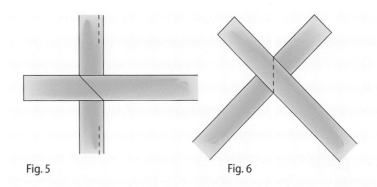

Fig. 5   Fig. 6

6. On final side, stop stitching about 10" (25.4 cm) short of starting point. Align unstitched start of binding along edge and fold at a 45-degree angle toward center of sandwich. Align and fold finishing tail of binding away from pillow top. Finger press both folds (Fig. 5).

7. Open both strips and place them right sides together, aligning creases on top of each other. Stitch along creased seam. Trim seam to ¼" (0.6 cm) (Fig. 6).

8. Fold binding over to back of sandwich, turning under ¼" (0.6 cm) edge; pin.

9. Hand stitch binding in place with matching thread or use a machine zigzag stitch to secure binding in place.

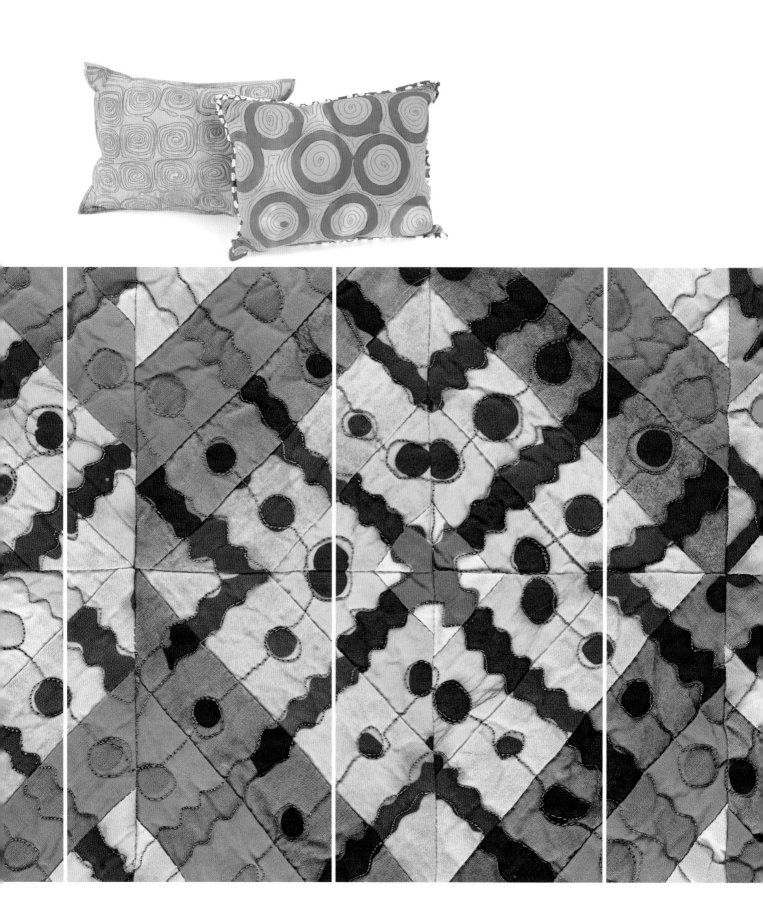

Chapter 7

Projects to Make

In the following pages, you'll find a dozen wonderful projects to make using your new patterned and dyed fabrics. Projects range from simple tableware items, to everyday personal accessories such as totes and camera straps, to pillow covers and—of course—a variety of quilts. I've placed the non-quilt projects first because they don't require a lot of fabric. You'll have a chance to get your feet wet quickly before committing to make the quantity of fabric you'll need for the larger projects.

Stripey Stripped Coasters

Finished size: approximately 6" (15.2 cm) square each

Leftover fabric is a fact of life in my studio, and when those extras are colorful striped batiks, I can't help but want to show them off. This is the perfect project for showcasing small bits of jewel-like fabric. They go together so quickly and easily that you'll have whipped up a set before your glasses begin to sweat.

Materials

Refer to Techniques for Adding Pattern to Fabric (page 20) and Basic Dyeing Technique (page 49) for guidance in preparing fabrics. This project uses fabrics patterned with the techniques described in Technique Three: Patterning with Brushes (page 39).

Note: Materials and instructions are for a set of four coasters.

Fabric

- Assorted small scraps of striped batik fabrics in various colors for coaster tops
- 4 squares, minimum 7" (17.8 cm), of coordinating fabric for coaster backs

Other Supplies

- Cotton batting: 4 squares, minimum 7" (17.8 cm)
- Hand sewing needle
- Iron and ironing surface
- Pins
- Quilter's ruler in size of choice
- Rotary cutter and mat
- Scissors
- Seam ripper
- Sewing machine
- Thread: neutral for sewing; coordinating color for machine quilting

Cutting

Measurements are approximate. Refer to A Few Sewing How-Tos (page 58) for additional guidance in freehand cutting.

From the assorted small scraps of striped batik fabrics, freehand cut a total of:

4 squares, 2" (5.1 cm)

Approximately 24–26 strips, each measuring about 1½" × 7" (3.8 cm × 17.8 cm)*

*I cut these so the stripes run across the width of the strips.

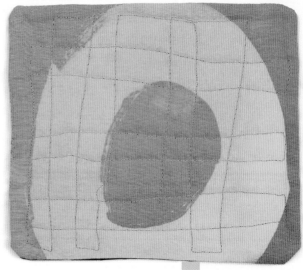

Use a colorful patterned fabric for the back and your coasters become reversible.

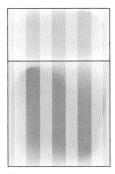

Fig. 1

Assembling Coasters

All seam allowances are ¼" (0.6 cm). Press all seams to one side. It's a good idea to alternate sides when seams intersect.

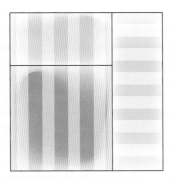

Fig. 2

1. With right sides together, sew one 1½" × 7" (3.8 cm × 17.8 cm) batik strip to one 2" (5.1 cm) square along one edge. Press. Trim strip even with edge of square (Fig. 1).

2. Turn unit 90 degrees and sew second, different-colored 1½" × 7" (3.8 cm × 17.8 cm) batik strip to adjacent side of unit. Press and trim (Fig. 2).

3. Continue to turn unit and sew strips around center square until unit measures approximately 6" (15.2 cm) square (Fig. 3).

4. Repeat steps 1–3 to make a total of four coaster tops.

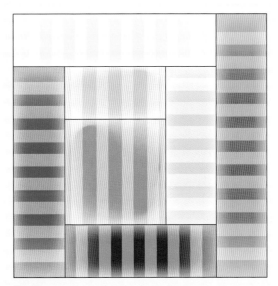

Fig. 3

Finishing Coasters

Refer to A Few Sewing How-Tos (page 58) for guidance with these finishing steps.

1. Using rotary cutter and quilter's ruler, straighten edges and square corners of each coaster top as necessary.

2. Layer batting, coaster backing (right side up), and coaster top (right side down). Pin layers together.

3. Trim backing and batting flush with coaster top.

4. Sew around perimeter of coaster sandwich ¼" (0.6 cm) from raw edges, leaving a 2" (5.1 cm) opening on one side for turning (Fig. 4).

5. Remove pins, trim excess seam fabric at corners, and turn coaster right side out.

6. Press coaster flat. Turn under and press ¼" (0.6 cm) seam allowance at opening.

7. With hand sewing needle and coordinating thread, slipstitch opening closed.

8. Quilt to secure all layers. Samples were machine quilted with orange thread following gridded pattern created by the stripes.

9. Repeat steps 2–8 to complete remaining three coasters.

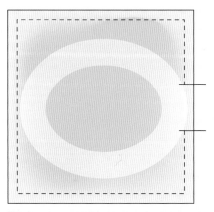

Fig. 4

A Place at the Table Ware

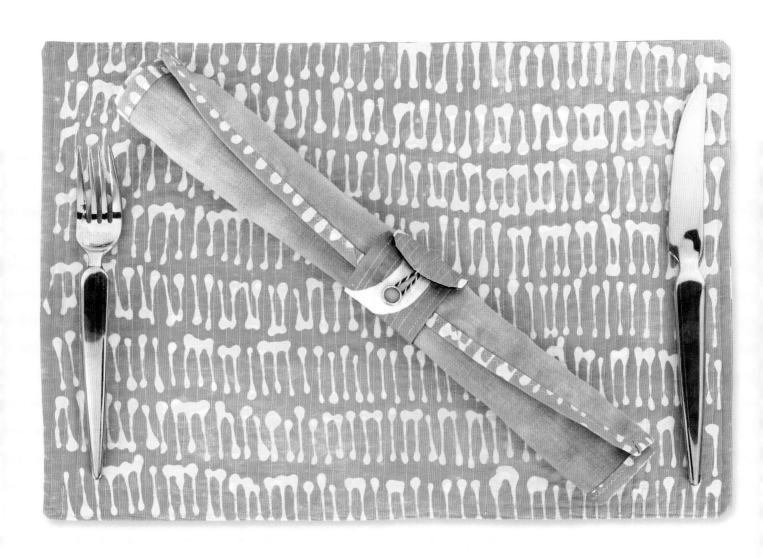

Finished sizes:
Placemat: 12" × 17" (30.5 cm × 43.2 cm)
Napkin: 13½" (34.3 cm) square
Napkin ring: 2" × 6" (5.1 cm × 15.2 cm)

This project was inspired by my desire to design a fabric napkin ring. I longed to make this item because I wanted to showcase one of my many vintage buttons. The napkin ring looked awfully forlorn by itself, though, so I created the placemat and napkin to go with it. Four place settings would make a wonderful gift.

Materials

Refer to Techniques for Adding Pattern to Fabric (page 20) and Basic Dyeing Technique (page 49) for guidance in preparing fabrics. The napkin ring uses fabrics patterned with the techniques described in Technique One: Stamping with Found Objects (page 26) and the placemat and napkin use fabrics patterned with the techniques described in Technique Two: Using Traditional Wax-Resist Tools (page 32).

Note: Materials and instructions are for one place setting.

Fabric

Placemat
- 1 piece each, 12½" × 17½" (31.8 cm × 44.5 cm), of two coordinating batik fabrics for placemat front and back
- 1 piece, 12½" × 17½" (31.8 cm × 44.5 cm), cotton muslin for filler

Napkin
- 1 square, 14" (35.6 cm), of hand-dyed linen for napkin
- 1½"-wide (3.8 cm) strips to total 42" (106.7 cm)

Napkin ring
- 1 piece each, 6½" × 2½" (16.5 cm × 6.4 cm), of two coordinating batik fabrics for napkin ring front and back

Use a fabric in a different color and pattern for the back of your placemat so you can turn it over for a whole new look.

Other Supplies

- Button, ½" (1.3 cm) diameter, for napkin ring
- Fabric marking pen
- Fusible interfacing
- Hand sewing needle
- Iron and ironing surface
- Pins
- Rotary cutter and mat
- Scissors
- Scrap cord, about 3" (7.6 cm), for napkin ring
- Spray starch (optional)
- Thread: neutral for sewing; coordinating color for topstitching

Fig. 1

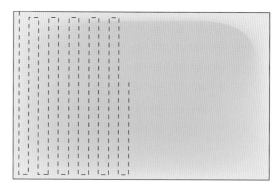

Fig. 2

Assembling Placemat

All seam allowances are ¼" (0.6 cm).

1. Place 12½" × 17½" (31.8 cm × 44.5 cm) placemat front and back, right sides together, on top of muslin. Pin. Sew layers together, leaving a 6" (15.2 cm) opening on one side for turning (Fig. 1).

2. Remove pins, trim excess seam fabric at corners, and turn placemat right side out.

3. Press placemat flat. Turn under and press ¼" (0.6 cm) seam allowance at opening.

4. Starting at one short edge, topstitch placemat with coordinating topstitching thread in parallel lines ¼" (0.6 cm) apart (Fig. 2). Topstitching will sew opening closed.

Making Napkin

Refer to A Few Sewing How-Tos (page 58) for guidance with binding.

1. Press 14" (35.6 cm) linen square with iron and spray starch. Spray starch stiffens the linen and makes it easier to work with.

2. Sew 1½"-wide (3.8 cm) binding strips together using diagonal seams. Press.

3. Using coordinating topstitching thread, sew binding to napkin, finishing with zigzag stitch.

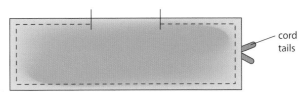

Fig. 4

cord
tails

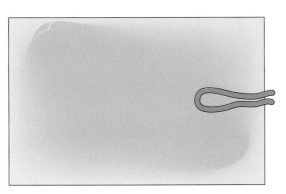

Fig. 3

Fig. 5

cord

Assembling Napkin Ring

1. Iron fusible interfacing onto wrong side of one 6½" × 2½" (16.5 cm × 6.4 cm) batik piece.

2. Place non-interfaced 6½" × 2½" (16.5 cm × 6.4 cm) batik piece right side up. Position scrap cord in center of fabric so that cord forms loop facing into center of fabric (Fig. 3).

3. Pin interfaced and non-interfaced fabric rectangles right sides together.

4. Sew rectangles together, making sure to catch tails of looped cord in stitching. Leave a 2" (5.1 cm) opening on one side for turning (Fig. 4).

5. Remove pins and turn napkin ring right side out, being careful to push out corners and cord.

6. Press napkin ring flat. Turn under and press ¼" (0.6 cm) seam allowance at opening.

7. Starting at one long edge, topstitch napkin ring with coordinating topstitching thread in parallel lines ¼" (0.6 cm) apart (Fig. 5). Topstitching will sew opening closed.

8. Overlap short edges of napkin ring about ½" (1.3 cm) and, with fabric marking pen, mark placement for button (Fig. 6).

9. Hand sew button in place.

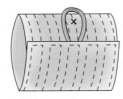

Fig. 6

TAKE NOTE

Sew a button on the underside of the napkin ring, and the ring becomes reversible.

On a Whim
Reversible Tote

Finished size: 16" × 15" × 4" (40.6 cm × 38.1 cm × 10.2 cm)

As a child, I was a huge fan of skorts because they were two things at the same time: a skirt and shorts. I've always loved reversible items for that same reason: getting two of something wrapped up in one.

This tote, like the skorts I wore as a 10-year-old, is more than it seems on the surface. Made with up to four different fabrics, it can be two completely different bags. Use it for work, shopping, or on your way to recess.

Materials

Refer to Techniques for Adding Pattern to Fabric (page 20) and Basic Dyeing Technique (page 49) for guidance in preparing fabrics. The various examples of this project use fabrics patterned with the techniques described in Technique One: Stamping with Found Objects (page 26) and Technique Three: Patterning with Brushes (page 39).

Note: Materials and instructions are for one reversible tote.

Fabric
- ½ yard (0.46 m) each of two different-colored and patterned batik fabrics for tote body (Fabric A and Fabric B)
- ¼ yard (0.23 m) each of two different-colored and patterned coordinating batik fabrics for tote straps (Fabric C and Fabric D)

Other Supplies
- Fabric marking pen
- Iron and ironing surface
- Iron-on interfacing: ⅝ yard (0.57 m), 18" (45.7 cm) wide
- Pins
- Quilter's ruler: 4" (10.2 cm) square; rectangle in size of choice
- Rotary cutter and mat
- Scissors
- Seam ripper
- Sewing machine
- Thread: neutral color for sewing; coordinating color for topstitching

Cutting

From Fabric A and Fabric B, cut:
2 pieces each, 16½" × 15½" (41.9 cm × 39.4 cm)
  (4 total)

From Fabric C and Fabric D, cut:
2 strips each, 2½" × 25" (6.4 cm × 63.5 cm)
  (4 total)

From the iron-on interfacing, cut:
2 strips, 2½" × 25" (6.4 cm × 63.5 cm)

Each *On a Whim Reversible Tote* shown on page 76 sports a whole new look when you turn it inside out.

Fig. 1

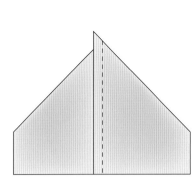

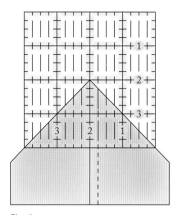

Fig. 2

Fig. 3

Assembling Tote Body

All seam allowances are ¼" (0.6 cm). Press all seams to one side. It's a good idea to alternate sides when seams intersect.

1. With right sides together, sew 16½" × 15½" (41.9 cm × 39.4 cm) Fabric A pieces together along both long sides and one short side (Fig. 1).

2. Repeat step 1 using 16½" × 15½" (41.9 cm × 39.4 cm) Fabric B pieces.

3. Fold bottom of unit from step 1 so one stitched corner forms triangle point (Fig. 2). Make sure that bottom and side seams bisect triangle from point to base.

4. Using 4" (10.2 cm) quilter's square ruler, measure 2" (5.1 cm) from point of triangle (Fig. 3). Mark base of triangle with fabric marking pen.

5. Pin and sew along marked line (Fig. 4).

6. Repeat steps 3–5 to fold, measure, mark, pin, and sew opposite bottom corner of tote unit from step 1.

7. Repeat steps 3–5 to fold, measure, mark, pin, and sew both bottom corners of tote unit from step 2.

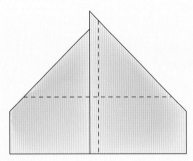

Fig. 4

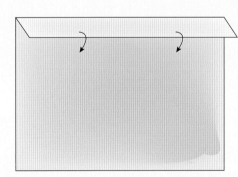

Fig. 5

8. Turn under and press ¼" (0.6 cm) hem to wrong side of top edge of tote unit from step 6 (Fig. 5). Repeat using tote unit from step 7. Set both units aside for now.

Making Tote Straps

1. Following manufacturer's instructions, iron one 2½" × 25" (6.4 cm × 63.5 cm) strip of interfacing onto wrong side of one 2½" × 25" (6.4 cm × 63.5 cm) Fabric C strip.

2. Place strip from step 1, fabric sides together, with 2½" × 25" (6.4 cm × 63.5 cm) Fabric D strip.

3. Sew strips together along long edges.

4. Turn strap right side out and press flat.

5. Starting approximately ¼" (0.6 cm) from one long edge, topstitch strap with coordinating topstitching thread in parallel lines ¼" (0.6 cm) apart (Fig. 6). Stop topstitching when last line measures approximately ¼" (0.6 cm) from opposite edge.

6. Repeat steps 1–5 to make second strap.

Fig. 6

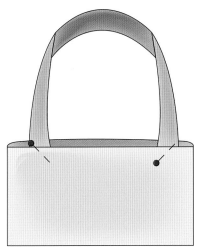

Fig. 7

Finishing Tote

1. With wrong sides together, place one tote body unit inside other tote body unit. Pin.

2. Insert ¼" (0.6 cm) of each end of one strap unit between tote bodies, about 2" (5.1 cm) from each side seam. Pin (Fig. 7). Repeat to insert and pin remaining strap unit to opposite side of tote.

3. Using a scant ¼" (0.6 cm) seam allowance, topstitch around top edge of tote bodies, securing straps in seam as you sew.

4. Sew second row of topstitching approximately ¼" (0.6) from first line of stitching.

Combine fabrics patterned with different techniques, or pair patterned fabrics with hand-dyed, non-patterned fabrics; the possibilities are endless.

Shutterbug
Camera Strap

Finished size: approximately 56½" (143.5 cm) long

One of the fringe benefits of patterning your own fabric is your ability to craft an amazing array of everyday items that are completely unique. You may have the same camera as your brother and your co-worker and your neighbor's girlfriend, but your camera strap is one-of-a-kind.

Materials

Refer to Techniques for Adding Pattern to Fabric (page 20) and Basic Dyeing Technique (page 49) for guidance in preparing fabrics. This project uses fabrics patterned with the techniques described in Technique Two: Using Traditional Wax-Resist Tools (page 32) and Technique Three: Patterning with Brushes (page 39).

Note: Materials and instructions are for one camera strap.

Fabric

- ⅛ yard (0.11 m) each of two different patterned batik fabrics (Fabric A for main strap and Fabric B for wedges and strips)*

In the sample, I used a chartreuse and green stamped batik for Fabric A and a pink and fuchsia striped batik for Fabric B.

Other Supplies

- Iron and ironing surface
- Ladderlocs (2)
- Lightweight iron-on interfacing: 2½" × 23½" (6.4 cm × 59.7 cm) strip
- Pins
- Quilter's ruler in size of choice
- Rotary cutter and mat
- Scissors
- Seam ripper
- Sewing machine
- Template material: 3" (7.6 cm) square
- Thread: neutral color for sewing; coordinating color for machine quilting

Camera strap in an
alternative colorway

Cutting

*Use template material and full-sized pattern on
page 87 to make template for wedge.*

From Fabric A, cut:
2 strips, 2½" × 23" (6.4 cm × 58.4 cm)

From Fabric B, cut:
4 wedge pieces
2 strips, 1½" × 16" (3.8 cm × 40.6 cm)

Fig. 1

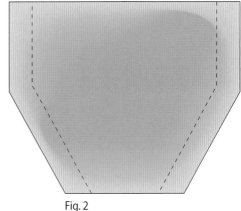

Fig. 2

Assembling Main Strap

All seam allowances are ¼" (0.6 cm).

1. Iron interfacing onto wrong side of one 2½" × 23" (6.4 cm × 58.4 cm) Fabric A strip.

2. Place remaining 2½" × 23" (6.4 cm × 58.4 cm) Fabric A strip right sides together with prepared strip from step 1. Stitch along both long edges.

3. Turn strap unit right side out. Press.

4. Starting approximately ¼" (0.6 cm) from one long edge, topstitch strap unit with coordinating topstitching thread in parallel lines ¼" (0.6 cm) apart. Stop topstitching when last line measures approximately ¼" (0.6 cm) from opposite edge (Fig. 1).

5. Place two Fabric B wedge pieces right sides together and sew, leaving openings along short edges (Fig. 2).

6. Turn wedge unit right side out.

7. Repeat steps 5 and 6 to make second wedge unit.

8. Slip ¼" (0.6 cm) of Fabric A strap into larger opening of Fabric B wedge (Fig. 3). Tuck in ¼" (0.6 cm) seam allowance at wedge piece opening. Press and pin.

9. Machine stitch opening closed (Fig. 4).

10. Repeat steps 8 and 9 on opposite end of Fabric A strap.

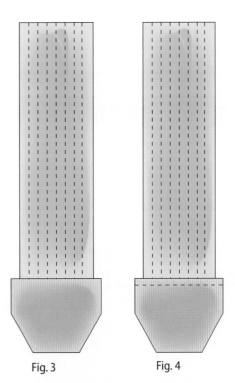

Fig. 3   Fig. 4

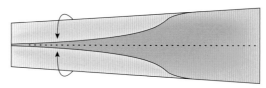

Fig. 6

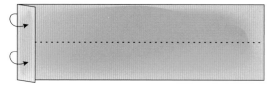

Fig. 5

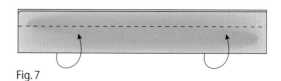

Fig. 7

Assembling and Adding Strips

1. With wrong sides together, fold one 1½" × 16" (3.8 cm × 40.6 cm) Fabric B strip in half lengthwise. Press.

2. Open folded strip. Fold under ¼" (0.6 cm) hem along both short sides (Fig. 5). Press.

3. Fold both long raw edges to center crease (Fig. 6). Press. Fold strip in half again and stitch (Fig. 7).

4. Repeat steps 1–3 to make second strip.

5. Slip ¼" (0.6 cm) of Fabric B strip into one wedge unit at smaller opening.

6. Tuck in ¼" (0.6 cm) seam allowance and machine stitch closed. Topstitch around perimeter of wedge unit about ¼" (0.6 cm) from edge (Fig. 8).

7. Repeat steps 5 and 6 with second Fabric B strip and opposite wedge unit.

Fig. 8

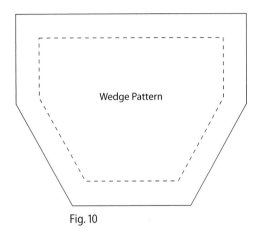

Fig. 10

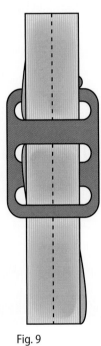

Fig. 9

Attaching Strap to Camera

1. Thread ladderloc through one Fabric B strip.

2. Wind strip through camera strap eyelet on camera and back through ladderloc (Fig. 9). Adjust length as desired.

3. Repeat steps 1 and 2 to attach second Fabric B strip to camera.

Show-Off Pillow Cover

Finished size: 12" × 16" (30.5 cm × 40.6 cm)

I call these "show-off" pillow covers because the focus is squarely on the beautiful fabric. The covers are whole cloth and the machine quilting outlines the patterning created with wax and dye. The slight modification in the shape of the pillows is just unique enough to add something special to a very simple project. I chose to make my pillow covers from fabric that was dyed, discharged, and overdyed because that, too, is a little out of the ordinary.

Materials

Refer to Techniques for Adding Pattern to Fabric (page 20) and Basic Dyeing Technique (page 49) for guidance in preparing fabrics. This project uses fabrics patterned with the techniques described in Technique One: Stamping with Found Objects (page 26), Technique Two: Using Traditional Wax-Resist Tools (page 32), and Technique Four: Discharging and Overdyeing (page 44).

Note: Materials and instructions are for one pillow cover.

Fabric

- ½ yard (0.46 m) of batik fabric for pillow top
- 1 piece, 14½" × 18½" (36.9 cm × 47.0 cm), of cotton muslin for pillow-top back
- ½ yard (0.46 m) of coordinating fabric batik fabric for pillow backing
- ⅛ yard (0.11 m) of a different coordinating batik fabric for binding

Other Supplies

- Basting materials
- Cotton batting: 1 piece, 14½" × 18½" (36.9 cm × 47.0 cm)
- Iron and ironing surface
- Pillow form: 12" × 16" (30.5 cm × 40.6 cm)
- Pins
- Quilter's ruler in size of choice
- Rotary cutter and mat
- Scissors
- Seam ripper
- Sewing machine with zipper foot attachment
- Thread: neutral for sewing; coordinating color for quilting
- Zipper: 12" (30.5 cm) standard in coordinating color

Fig. 1

Cutting

From the batik fabric for pillow top, cut:
1 piece, 12½" × 16½" (31.8 cm × 41.9 cm)

From the coordinating batik fabric for pillow backing, cut:
2 pieces, 12½" × 14" (31.8 cm × 35.6 cm)

From the coordinating batik fabric for binding, cut:
1½"-wide (3.8 cm) strips to total 70" (177.8 cm)

Quilting Pillow Top

1. Layer muslin piece, batting, and 12½" × 16½" (31.8 cm × 41.9 cm) piece of pillow top fabric (right side up). Baste layers together using your preferred method.

2. Quilt to secure all layers. The samples were machine quilted with contrasting thread to outline fabric patterning.

3. Trim batting and muslin flush with pillow top.

Creating Pillow Back

All seam allowances are ¼" (0.6 cm). Press all seams to one side.

1. Place one 12½" × 14" (31.8 cm × 35.6 cm) pillow backing piece, wrong side up, on ironing surface. Turn and press ¼" (0.6 cm) hem, wrong sides together, along one short side (Fig. 1).

2. Repeat to press 1" (2.5 cm) hem along same short side (Fig. 2).

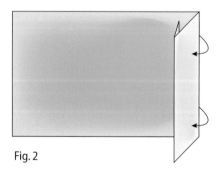

Fig. 2

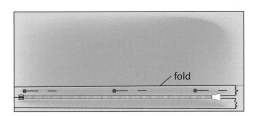

Fig. 3

3. Pin closed zipper, wrong side up, to pressed edge, aligning tape edge of zipper with *inner* folded edge of backing piece (Fig. 3). (Zipper is slightly shorter than fabric edge.) Make sure zipper doesn't extend beyond edge of fabric running perpendicular to fold.

4. Using a machine zipper foot, sew zipper to backing piece.

5. Repeat step 1 to prepare remaining 12½" × 14" (31.8 cm × 35.6 cm) backing piece, and steps 3 and 4 to pin and sew zipper in place, this time aligning zipper so teeth extend just beyond *outer* folded edge of backing piece (Fig. 4).

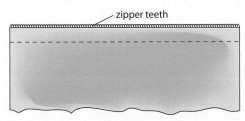

Fig. 4

Assembling Pillow Cover

Refer to A Few Sewing How-Tos (page 58) for guidance with these finishing steps.

1. With backing pieces zippered together, layer backing (wrong side up) and pillow top (right side up) on cutting mat, centering zippered backing beneath pillow top. If zipper needs trimming, trim on end opposite zipper pull. Keep zipper closed while trimming. Pin.

2. Trim edges of pillow back flush with quilted pillow top.

3. Sew 1½"-wide (3.8 cm) binding strips together using diagonal seams. Press.

4. Sew binding to pillow cover with ¼" (0.6 cm) seam.

5. Insert pillow form.

Ovals Pillow Cover

Finished size: approximately 20" × 18" (50.8 cm × 45.7 cm)

If I had to name the single greatest influence on the textiles that I make, it would be other textiles. Whether it is an African Kuba cloth or an Indian sari, nothing inspires me more than other fiber creations. The design for this pillow cover owes a great debt to the amazing work of the Bauhaus weavers, especially Anni Albers. Its simple, graphic shapes and colors really place the batik fabric at center stage.

Materials

Refer to Techniques for Adding Pattern to Fabric (page 20) and Basic Dyeing Technique (page 49) for guidance in preparing fabrics. This project uses fabrics patterned with the techniques described in Technique One: Stamping with Found Objects (page 26) and Technique Four: Discharging and Overdyeing (page 44).

Fabric

- ½ yard (0.46 m) each of two oval-stamped batik fabrics in similar colors for pillow top
- 1 square, 25" (63.5 cm), of cotton muslin for pillow-top back
- ¾ yard (0.69 m) of coordinating hand-dyed or purchased fabric for pillow back and binding

Other Supplies

- Basting materials
- Buttons: 3 (½" [1.3 cm] diameter)
- Cotton batting: 25" (63.5 cm) square
- Fabric marking pen
- Iron and ironing surface
- Pillow form: 18" (45.7 cm) square or 20" (50.8 cm) square*
- Pins
- Quilter's ruler in size of choice
- Rotary cutter and mat
- Scissors
- Seam ripper
- Sewing machine
- Thread: neutral for sewing; contrasting color for quilting

*Will depend upon how full you like your pillow.

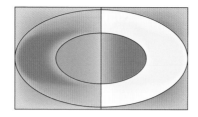

Fig. 1

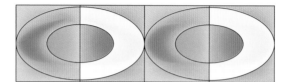

Fig. 2

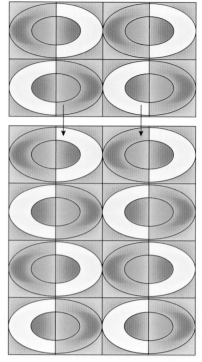

Fig. 3

Cutting

Cut the oval-stamped pieces in this pillow cover freehand; that is, put your rulers away and cut the pieces from the fabric with just a rotary cutter. Don't panic; the shapes don't need to be exact. Remember to add about ¼" (0.6 cm) for seam allowance all around. Refer to A Few Sewing How-Tos (page 58) for additional guidance in freehand cutting.

From each ½ yard (0.46 m) of oval-stamp batik fabric, cut:
24 half oval pieces, 3½" × 3" (8.9 cm × 7.6 cm)

From the coordinating fabric, cut:
2 pieces, 20½" × 12" (52.1 cm × 30.5 cm)
1½"-wide (3.8 cm) strips to total 85" (215.9 cm)

Assembling Pillow Top

All seam allowances are ¼" (0.6 cm). Press all seams to one side. It's a good idea to alternate sides when seams intersect.

1. Sort 3½" × 3" (8.9 cm × 7.6 cm) pieces into two stacks, one of each color.

2. Take one piece from each stack and place right sides together. Sew pieces together along edge with open half oval (Fig. 1). Press. Make 24.

3. Place two units from step 2 right sides together with colors opposite. Sew along one short edge (Fig. 2). Press. Make 12.

4. Repeat to sew pairs into groups of four, then eights, then twelves, pressing as you go (Fig. 3). Make two.

5. With right sides together, sew units from step 4 together along one long edge (Fig. 4). Press.

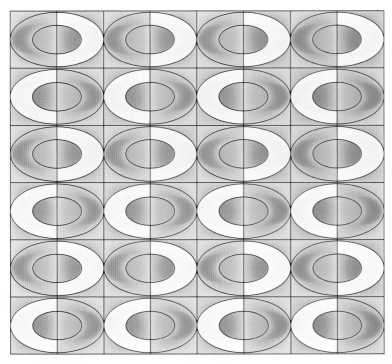

Fig. 4

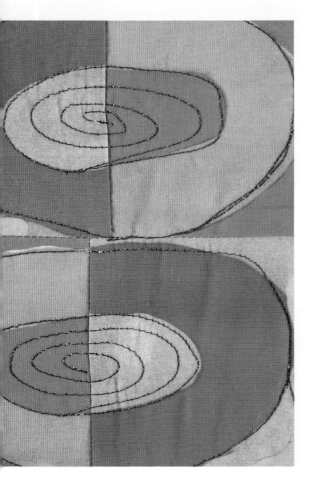

Quilting Pillow Top

Refer to A Few Sewing How-Tos (page 58) for guidance with layering and basting.

1. Layer muslin square, batting, and pillow top (right side up). Baste layers together using your preferred method.

2. Quilt to secure all layers. The sample was machine quilted with orange thread concentrically inside circles and to outline circles.

3. Trim batting and backing flush with pillow top.

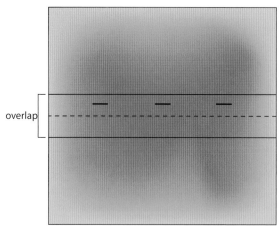

overlap

Fig. 5

Assembling Pillow

All seam allowances are ¼" (0.6 cm). Press all seams to one side.

1. Fold ¼" (0.6 cm) under along one long side of each 20½" × 12" (52.1 cm × 30.5 cm) backing piece. Press. Fold under 1" (2.5 cm) on same edge of each piece and press.

2. Topstitch, making sure to catch the ¼" (0.6 cm) fold. You will use these edges for buttons and buttonholes.

3. Make three evenly spaced button-holes along long folded sewn edge of one pillow back piece. Use your selected buttons as a guide to size buttonholes.

4. Using seam ripper, open buttonholes.

5. Place quilted pillow top (right side down) on your cutting mat. Place back-ing pieces (right side up) on top of pillow top, with buttonhole piece overlapping on top center (Fig. 5). Pin. Carefully turn pillow cover over and trim edges of pil-low back flush with quilted pillow top.

Finishing Pillow

Refer to A Few Sewing How-Tos (page 58) for guidance with these finishing steps.

1. Sew 1½"-wide (3.8 cm) binding strips together using diagonal seams. Press.

2. Sew binding to pillow cover with ¼" (0.6 cm) seam.

3. Using fabric marking pen, mark placement for buttons and hand sew to button band.

4. Insert pillow form.

What's on Top Mini-Quilt

Finished size: approximately 19" × 22" (48.3 cm × 55.9 cm)

This mini-quilt relies on stripes, cut and sewn freehand, to create a plaid-like surface. Depending on your perspective, the light, or even your color preferences, different areas appear to come forward while others recede. A pillow-slip finishing technique emphasizes the wonkiness of this quilt and further blurs "what's on top."

Materials

Refer to Techniques for Adding Pattern to Fabric (page 20) and Basic Dyeing Technique (page 49) for guidance in preparing fabrics. This project uses fabrics patterned with the techniques described in Technique Three: Patterning with Brushes (page 39).

Fabric
- ⅛ yard (0.11 m) each of 8–10 striped batik fabrics in various colors for blocks
- ¾ yard (0.69 m) coordinating fabric for backing

Other Supplies
- Basting materials
- Cotton batting: 22" × 25" piece (55.9 cm × 63.5 cm)*
- Hand sewing needle
- Iron and ironing surface
- Pins
- Quilter's ruler in size of choice
- Rotary cutter and mat
- Scissors
- Seam ripper
- Sewing machine
- Thread: neutral and matching color for sewing; coordinating color for quilting

You may want a slightly larger piece if you plan to hand quilt using a hoop.

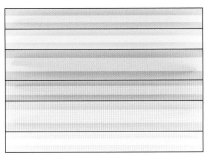

Fig. 1

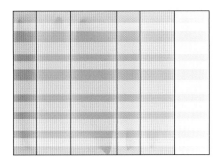

Fig. 2

Cutting

Refer to A Few Sewing How-Tos (page 58) for additional guidance in freehand cutting.

From the 8–10 striped batik fabrics, freehand cut a total of:

Approximately 30 strips, each measuring about 2" × 7" (5.1 cm × 17.8 cm), cut with the stripes running down the strip length (A strips)

Approximately 30 strips, each measuring about 2" × 7" (5.1 cm × 17.8 cm), cut with the stripes running across the strip width (B strips)

Assembling Blocks

All seam allowances are ¼" (0.6 cm). Press all seams to one side. It's a good idea to alternate sides when seams intersect. Due to the improvisational nature of this project, your quilt size may vary. You may also have a few strips left over.

1. With right sides together, sew six different A strips together along their long edges. Press. Trim block so that edges are even and label them A blocks (Fig. 1). Make a total of four A blocks.

2. Repeat step 1 using six different B strips (Fig. 2). Label them B blocks. Make a total of five B blocks.

TAKE NOTE

If blocks are not the same size, delete a strip or add a piece and trim after sewing.

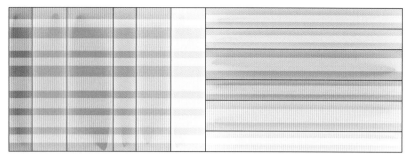

Fig. 3

Assembling Quilt

1. With right sides together, sew one A block and one B block together (Fig. 3). Press.

2. Repeat step 1 to make a total of three pairs.

3. With right sides together, sew three pairs from step 2 together along their long edges (Fig. 4). Press and trim as needed.

4. With right sides together, sew remaining B block between remaining A blocks (Fig. 4). Press.

5. Arrange and sew units from steps 3 and 4 together. Press.

Fig. 4

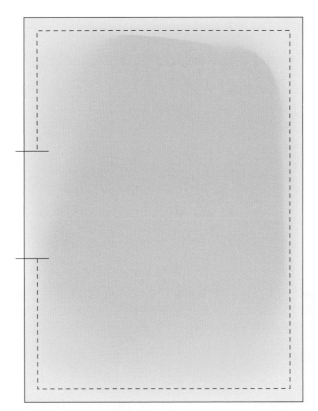

Fig. 5

Finishing Quilt

Refer to A Few Sewing How-Tos (page 58) for guidance with these finishing steps.

1. Using rotary cutter and ruler, straighten edges and square corners of quilt top as necessary.

2. Layer cotton batting, quilt backing (right side up), and quilt top (right side down). Pin layers together.

3. Trim backing and batting flush with quilt top.

4. Sew around perimeter of quilt sandwich ¼" (0.6 cm) from raw edges, leaving a 9" (22.9 cm) opening on one side for turning (Fig. 5).

5. Remove pins, trim excess seam fabric at corners, and turn quilt right side out. Press, making sure to push corners and edges out completely.

6. Turn under and press ¼" (0.6 cm) seam allowance at opening. With hand sewing needle and matching thread, slipstitch opening closed.

7. Baste layers together using your preferred method.

8. Quilt to secure all layers. The sample was machine quilted with yellow thread following edges of vertical dyed stripes, from top to bottom, and pieced seams from side to side.

Twinkle Appliqué Quilt

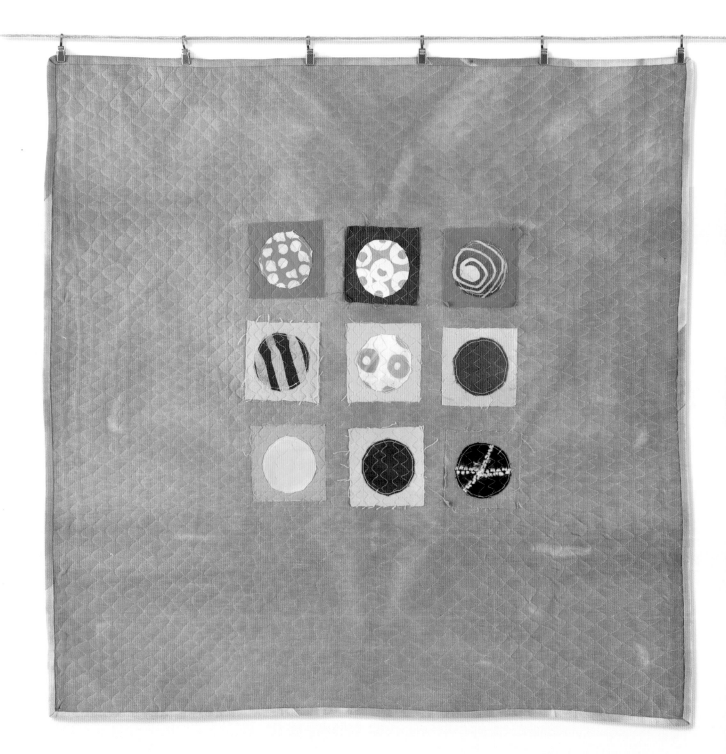

Finished size: 31" (78.7 cm) square

Anyone who's ever watched the *Sesame Street* character, Telly Monster, expound on his love of triangles can relate to my passion for circles. Circles have been the starting point for many of my quilts, pillows, and fabric designs. Once again I've turned, no pun intended, to this shape as a focal point for this quilt. The design allows you to feature a few treasured fabrics and highlight the richness of color only available with hand-dyed fabrics.

Materials

Refer to Techniques for Adding Pattern to Fabric (page 20) and Basic Dyeing Technique (page 49) for guidance in preparing fabrics. This project uses fabrics patterned with the techniques described in Technique Two: Using Traditional Wax-Resist Tools (page 32).

Fabric

- 1 square each, 3½" (8.9 cm), of nine different hand-dyed and/or batik fabrics for circles
- 1 square each, 3½" (8.9 cm), of nine different-colored hand-dyed fabric for squares
- 1 yard (0.91 m) of hand-dyed cotton or linen for background
- 1 yard (0.91 m) of coordinating fabric for backing
- ¼ yard (0.23 m) of second coordinating fabric for binding

Other Supplies

- Basting materials
- Basting tape or fabric glue
- Cotton batting: 36" (91.4 cm) square*
- Iron and ironing surface
- Pins
- Quilter's ruler in size of choice
- Rotary cutter and mat
- Scissors
- Seam ripper
- Sewing machine
- Template material: 3½" (8.9 cm) square
- Thread: neutral for sewing; coordinating color for quilting

You may want a slightly larger piece if you plan to hand quilt using a hoop.

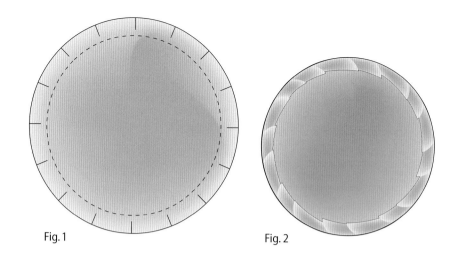

Fig. 1

Fig. 2

Cutting

Use template material and full-sized pattern on page 105 to make template for circle.

From each of the nine different hand-dyed and/or batik fabrics for circles, cut:
1 circle piece

From the hand-dyed cotton or linen for background, cut:
1 square, 31" (78.7 cm)

From the coordinating fabric for binding, cut:
1½"-wide (3.8 cm) strips to total approximately 135" (342.9 cm)

Assembling Quilt Top

1. Machine stitch ¼" (0.6 cm) from raw edge around perimeter of one fabric circle. Cut notches every ¼" (0.6 cm) into raw edge, taking care not to cut into stitching (Fig. 1).

2. Press notched seam allowance to wrong side of circle (Fig. 2).

3. Center and pin circle, right side up, to right side of one 3½" (8.9 cm) hand-dyed square.

4. Machine stitch circle to square using a scant ¼" (0.6 cm) seam allowance (Fig. 3).

5. Repeat steps 1–4 using remaining eight circles and squares.

6. Using either basting tape or fabric glue, baste circle/square units to 31" (78.7 cm) background fabric in three rows of three units each, leaving approximately 1" (2.5 cm) between units (Fig. 4).

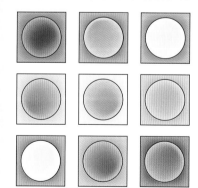

Fig. 4

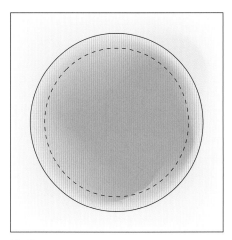

Fig. 3

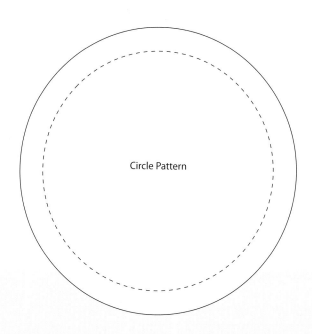

Circle Pattern

Finishing Quilt

Refer to A Few Sewing How-Tos (page 58) for guidance with these finishing steps.

1. Layer backing, batting, and quilt top. Baste layers together using your preferred method.

2. Quilt to secure all layers. The sample was machine quilted with light blue thread in an overall tight squiggly pattern that runs top to bottom over quilt surface.

3. Trim batting and backing flush with quilt top.

4. Sew 1½"-wide (3.8 cm) binding strips together using diagonal seams. Press.

5. Sew binding to quilt with ¼" (0.6 cm) seam.

The overall squiggly quilting, which resembles fish scales, permanently secures the blocks to the quilt.

Wide Stripes Quilt

Finished size: approximately 26" × 31" (66.0 cm × 78.7 cm)

I've often heard knitters say how the material—in their case, the yarn—guides their choice of pattern. I think this is true in quilting as well, especially when you pattern and dye the fabric yourself. In this straightforward quilt, the wide stripes seemed destined to come together as they did. But that doesn't mean that the fabric pattern functions as absolute dictator. Assert your personality by customizing the design with your own pattern and palette.

Materials

Refer to Techniques for Adding Pattern to Fabric (page 20) and Basic Dyeing Technique (page 49) for guidance in preparing fabrics. This project uses fabrics patterned with the techniques described in Technique Three: Patterning with Brushes (page 39).

Fabric

- ½ yard (0.46 m) each of six striped batik fabrics in various colors for blocks
- ½ yard (0.46 m) of a seventh striped batik fabric for blocks and border
- 1 yard (0.91 m) of coordinating fabric for backing

Other Supplies

- Cotton batting: 30" × 35" (76.2 cm × 88.9 cm)*
- Hand sewing needle
- Iron and ironing surface
- Pins
- Quilter's ruler in size of choice
- Rotary cutter and mat
- Scissors
- Seam ripper
- Sewing machine
- Thread: neutral and matching color for sewing; coordinating color for quilting

*You may want a slightly larger piece if you plan to hand quilt using a hoop.

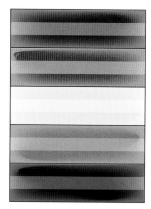

Fig. 1

Cutting

Refer to A Few Sewing How-Tos (page 58) for additional guidance in freehand cutting.

From *all seven* striped batik fabrics, freehand cut a total of:

10–12 strips, each measuring approximately 3" × 12" (7.6 cm × 30.5 cm), cut with the stripes running down the strip length (A strips)

10–12 strips, each measuring approximately 2½" × 14" (6.4 cm × 35.6 cm), cut with the stripes running across the strip width (B strips)

From the rest of the seventh striped batik fabric, freehand cut:

2 strips, 3" (7.6 cm) wide to total approximately 30" (76.2 cm), cut with the stripes running across the strip width (C strips)*

2 strips, 3" (7.6 cm) wide to total approximately 30" (76.2 cm), cut with the stripes running down the strip length (D strips)*

You might prefer to wait until the center of the quilt is assembled before cutting these strips. You may need to piece strips to achieve the desired length.

Assembling Quilt Top

All seam allowances are ¼" (0.6 cm). Press all seams to one side. It's a good idea to alternate sides when seams intersect. Due to the improvisational nature of this project, your quilt size may vary. You may also have a few strips left over.

1. With rights sides together, sew five different A strips together along their long edges (Fig. 1). Press and label them A blocks. Make two.

2. Repeat step 1 using five different B strips (Fig. 2). Make two and label them B blocks.

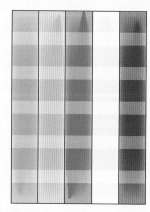

Fig. 2

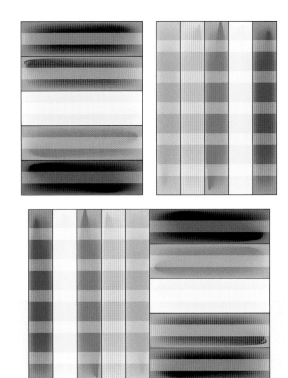

Fig. 3

Assembling Quilt

1. Arrange A and B blocks into two horizontal rows of two blocks each, turning blocks as shown (Fig. 3). Sew blocks into rows. Press. Sew rows together. Press.

2. Using a straight seam, sew together border strips with stripes running perpendicular to long edge.

3. Measure quilt from top to bottom. Sew C strips together with straight seams if necessary to achieve necessary length *or* trim a single 30" (76.2 cm) strip to fit. Make two borders and sew one to each long side of quilt top. Press away from borders.

4. Measure quilt from side to side. Sew D strips together with straight seams if necessary to achieve necessary length *or* trim single 30" (76.2 cm) strip to fit. Make two borders and sew one to each short side of quilt top (Fig. 4). Press.

TAKE NOTE

If blocks are not the same size, delete a strip or add a piece and trim after seaming.

Fig. 4

Finishing Quilt

Refer to A Few Sewing How-Tos (page 58) for guidance with these finishing steps.

1. Layer cotton batting, quilt backing (right side up), and quilt top (right side down). Pin layers together.

2. Trim backing and batting flush with quilt top.

3. Sew around perimeter of quilt sandwich ¼" (0.6 cm) from raw edges, leaving a 9" (22.9 cm) opening on one side for turning.

4. Remove pins, trim excess seam fabric at corners, and turn quilt right side out. Press, making sure to push corners and edges out completely.

5. Turn under and press ¼" (0.6 cm) seam allowance at opening. With hand sewing needle and matching thread, slipstitch gap closed.

6. Baste layers together using your preferred method.

7. Quilt to secure all layers. The sample was machine quilted with golden yellow/orange thread following vertical and horizontal lines created by batik fabrics.

Brisas del Mar Quilt

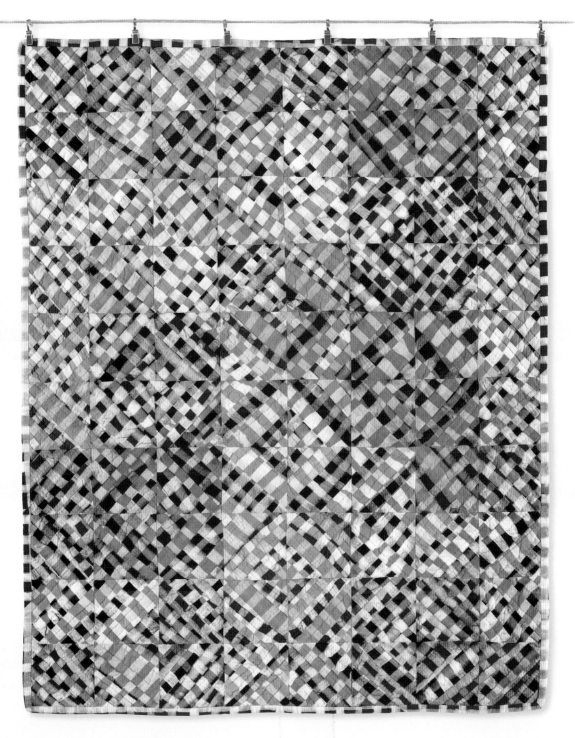

Finished size: 28" × 35" (71.1 cm × 88.9 cm)

The inspiration for this quilt came from a beautifully tiled pool in Mexico. In trying to recreate the mosaic quality of the tile, I relied on the transparency of the dyes and simple, but effective, piecing. Once the fabrics were patterned and dyed to create a plaid effect, I cut them into strips and re-pieced them. In crafting your own version, consider experimenting with different color combinations to create a unique quilted mosaic.

Materials

Refer to Techniques for Adding Pattern to Fabric (page 20) and Basic Dyeing Technique (page 49) for guidance in preparing fabrics. This project uses fabrics patterned with the techniques described in Technique Three: Patterning with Brushes (page 39).

Fabric

- 2¼ yards (2.06 m) of plaid batik in one color for blocks (Fabric A)
- 2¼ yards (2.06 m) of plaid batik in second color for blocks (Fabric B)
- 1 yard (0.91 m) of coordinating fabric for backing
- ¼ yard (0.23 m) of a different coordinating fabric for binding

Other Supplies

- Basting materials
- Cotton batting: 32" × 40" (81.2 cm × 101.6 cm)*
- Iron and ironing surface
- Pins
- Quilter's ruler: 4" (10.2 cm) square; rectangle in size of choice
- Rotary cutter and mat
- Scissors
- Seam ripper
- Sewing machine
- Thread: neutral color for sewing; coordinating color for quilting

*You may want a slightly larger piece if you plan to hand quilt using a hoop.

Cutting

Refer to A Few Sewing How-Tos (page 58) for additional guidance in freehand cutting.

From Fabric A, freehand cut:
240 strips, 1½" × 8" (3.8 cm × 20.3 cm)

From Fabric B, freehand cut:
240 strips, 1½" × 8" (3.8 cm × 20.3 cm)

From the coordinating fabric for binding, cut:
1½"-wide (3.8 cm) strips to total 140"
   (355.6 cm)

Assembling Blocks

All seam allowances are ¼" (0.6 cm). Press all seams to one side. It's a good idea to alternate sides when seams intersect.

1. With right sides together, sew six strips together—alternating Fabric A with Fabric B—along their long edges (Fig. 1). Press to one side. Stagger placement of strips so that similarly colored parts of strips do not align.

2. Place quilter's square ruler on point on sewn strips. Trim edges of block flush with ruler (Fig. 2).

3. Repeat steps 1 and 2 to make a total of 80 blocks.

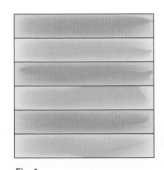

Fig. 1

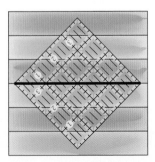

Fig. 2

Assembling Quilt

Arrange blocks into 10 horizontal rows of eight blocks each, turning the blocks as shown (Fig. 3). Sew blocks into rows. Press. Sew rows together. Press.

Finishing Quilt

Refer to A Few Sewing How-Tos (page 58) for guidance with these finishing steps.

1. Layer backing, batting, and quilt top. Baste layers together using your preferred method.

2. Quilt to secure all layers. The sample was hand quilted with white thread to accentuate the vertical zigzag created by the patches.

3. Trim batting and backing flush with quilt top.

4. Sew 1½"-wide (3.8 cm) binding strips together using diagonal seams. Press.

5. Sew binding to quilt with ¼" (0.6 cm) seam.

Fig. 3

Shoo Fly Bed Quilt

Finished size: 58½" × 87¾" (148.6 cm × 222.9 cm)

This design allowed me to work with a variety of fabrics patterned by using multiple techniques and featuring a variety of different colorways. Even the background areas are kept interesting and surprising with the use of several different white and near-white fabrics. A fairly large block size (9¾" [24.8 cm] square finished) adds to the quilt's contemporary feel. You can work with my color scheme or select one that suits your personal taste.

Materials

Refer to Techniques for Adding Pattern to Fabric (page 20) and Basic Dyeing Technique (page 49) for guidance in preparing fabrics. This project uses fabrics patterned with the techniques described in Technique One: Stamping with Found Objects (page 26), Technique Two: Using Traditional Wax-Resist Tools (page 32), Technique Three: Patterning with Brushes (page 39), and Technique Four: Discharging and Overdyeing (page 44).

Fabric

- 4 yards (3.66 m) total of assorted batik fabrics in various colors for block
- 2½ yards (2.29 m) total of assorted white or near-white cottons and linens for blocks
- 5¼ yards (4.80 m) of coordinating fabric for backing
- ½ yard (0.46 m) of coordinating fabric for binding

Other Supplies

- Basting materials
- Cotton batting: 63" × 92" (160.0 cm × 233.7 cm)
- Fabric marking pen
- Iron and ironing surface
- Pins
- Quilter's ruler in size of choice
- Rotary cutter and mat
- Scissors
- Seam ripper
- Sewing machine
- Thread: neutral for sewing; coordinating color for quilting

The quilting in the center of each block is enhanced with a freeform swirling motif.

Cutting

From the assorted batik fabrics, cut a total of:
224 squares, 3¾" (9.5 cm)*
112 squares, 4¼" (10.8 cm)*

From the assorted white and near-white fabrics, cut a total of:
56 squares, 3¾" (9.5 cm)**
112 squares, 4¼" (10.8 cm)**

From the coordinating fabric for binding, cut:
1½"-wide (3.8 cm) strips to total
   approximately 305" (774.7 cm)

*Cut these in matching sets of two 4¼"
(10.8 cm) squares and four 3¾" (9.5 cm)
squares.*
**Cut these in matching sets of two 4¼"
(10.8 cm) squares and one 3¾" (9.5 cm)
square.*

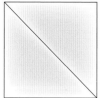
Fig. 1

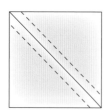
Fig. 2

Fig. 3

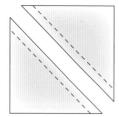
Fig. 4

Assembling Blocks

All seam allowances are ¼" (0.6 cm). Press all seams to one side. It's a good idea to alternate sides when seams intersect. In the following directions, the hand-dyed and patterned fabrics will be referred to as "patterned" and the white and near-white fabrics will be referred to as "white."

1. Place 4¼" (10.8 cm) patterned square and 4¼" (10.8 cm) white square right sides together. Pin.

2. Using fabric marker, draw diagonal line from corner to corner on wrong side of white square (Fig. 1).

3. Sew ¼" (0.6 cm) from both sides of marked line (Fig. 2).

4. Cut square in half on marked line to make two half-square-triangle units (Fig. 3). Press toward patterned fabric. Trim each unit to measure 3¾" (9.5 cm) square (Fig. 4).

5. Repeat steps 1–4 using a matching patterned square and matching white square to make two additional half-square-triangle units.

6. Arrange the four matching half-square-triangle units, four matching 3¾" (9.5 cm) patterned squares, and one matching 3¾" (9.5 cm) white square as shown (Fig. 5). Sew units and squares into rows. Press. Sew rows together. Press.

7. Repeat steps 1–6 using remaining patterned and white squares to make a total of 56 blocks.

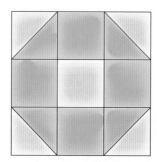
Fig. 5

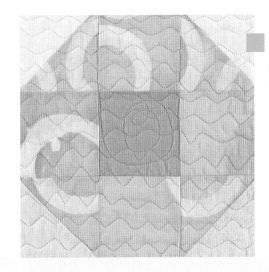

For variety, replace an occasional white square with a different "white" fabric.

Assembling Quilt Top

Arrange blocks into nine horizontal rows of six blocks each. Sew blocks into rows. Press. Sew rows together (Fig. 6). Press.

Finishing Quilt

Refer to A Few Sewing How-Tos (page 58) for guidance with these finishing steps.

1. Divide backing fabric in half crosswise (selvage to selvage), remove selvages, and sew together to make backing piece approximately 84" × 94¼" (213.4 cm × 239.4 cm).

2. Layer backing, batting, and quilt top. Baste layers together using your preferred method.

3. Quilt to secure all layers. The sample was machine quilted in off-white thread in an overall wavy pattern, with the center of each block enhanced with a freeform swirl.

4. Trim batting and backing flush with quilt top.

5. Sew 1½"-wide (3.8 cm) binding strips together using diagonal seams. Press.

6. Sew binding to quilt with ¼" (0.6 cm) seam.

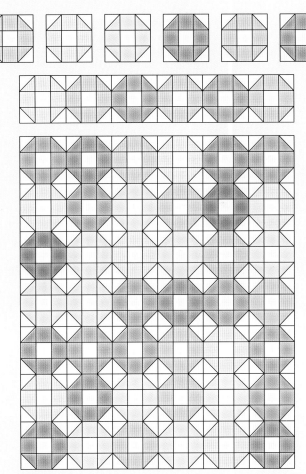

Fig. 6

E Block Quilt

Finished size: 28" × 35" (71.1 cm × 88.9 cm)

My neighbor, Elizabeth, found a wooden fabric-stamping block, shown on page 122, for a few dollars at a garage sale. It is a wonderful example of a traditional Indian fabric stamp, featuring a large gridded design and a nice sturdy handle. Within days I had patterned and dyed yards of fabric in multiple colorways using this block—and my *E Block Quilt* was born. You, too, can make a version of this quilt. All it takes to create the fabric is a wooden block with a grid-like pattern, wax, and dye.

Materials

Refer to Techniques for Adding Pattern to Fabric (page 20) and Basic Dyeing Technique (page 49) for guidance in preparing fabrics. This project uses fabrics patterned with the techniques described in Technique Two: Using Traditional Wax-Resist Tools (page 32).

Fabric

- ¼ yard (0.23 m) each of 8–10 grid-patterned batik fabrics in various colors for blocks
- 1 yard (0.91 m) of coordinating fabric for backing
- ¼ yard (0.23 m) of a different coordinating fabric for binding

Other Supplies

- Basting materials
- Cotton batting: 32" × 40" (81.3 cm × 101.6 cm)*
- Iron and ironing surface
- Pins
- Quilter's ruler: 4" (10.2 cm) square; rectangle in size of choice
- Rotary cutter and mat
- Scissors
- Seam ripper
- Sewing machine
- Thread: neutral for sewing; coordinating color for quilting

You may want a slightly larger piece if you plan to hand quilt using a hoop.

Cutting

Refer to A Few Sewing How-Tos (page 58) for additional guidance in freehand cutting.

From the 8–10 grid-patterned batik fabric, freehand cut a total of:
Approximately 480 strips, 1½" × 8" (3.8 cm × 20.3 cm), cut with wavy stripes running across the strip width

From the coordinating fabric for binding, cut:
1½"-wide (3.8 cm) strips to total 140" (355.6 cm)

I used this traditional wooden stamp to pattern the fabric for my *E Block Quilt*.

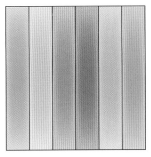

Fig. 1

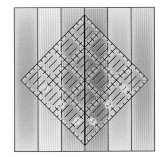

Fig. 2

Assembling Blocks

All seam allowances are ¼" (0.6 cm). Press all seams to one side. It's a good idea to alternate sides when seams intersect.

1. Divide 1½" × 8" (3.8 cm × 20.3 cm) batik strips into mixed-colored groupings of six strips each.

2. With right sides together, sew strips from one six-strip group together along their long edges (Fig. 1). Press.

3. Place quilter's square ruler on point on sewn strips. Trim edges of block flush with ruler (Fig. 2). *Note:* In order to achieve the overall gridded effect in the quilt top as shown on page 120, it is important that a wavy grid line run diagonally through the center of each block.

4. Repeat steps 2 and 3 to make a total of four blocks.

5. With right sides together, sew blocks together in pairs as shown (Fig. 3). Press. Sew pairs together (Fig. 4). Press. *Note:* Since strips were cut freehand, all strips may not line up perfectly.

6. Repeat steps 2–5 to make a total of 20 blocks.

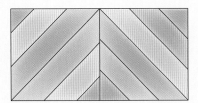

Fig. 3

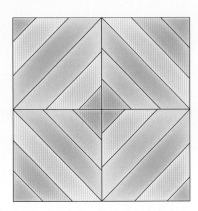

Fig. 4

Assembling Quilt Top

Arrange blocks into five horizontal rows of four blocks each. Sew blocks into rows. Press. Sew rows together (Fig. 5). Press.

Finishing Quilt

Refer to A Few Sewing How-Tos (page 58) for guidance with these finishing steps.

1. Layer backing, batting, and quilt top. Baste layers together using your preferred method.

2. Quilt to secure all layers. The sample was machine quilted with aqua thread to outline the circles and wavy gridded design.

3. Trim batting and backing flush with pillow top.

4. Sew 1½"-wide (3.8 cm) binding strips together using diagonal seams. Press.

5. Sew binding to quilt with ¼" (0.6 cm) seam.

Fig. 5

About the Author

Born in Israel, Malka Dubrawsky grew up in Houston, Texas, and attended the University of Texas at Austin. She earned a Bachelor of Fine Arts in Studio Art and went on to start A Stitch in Dye, a business focused on crafting a variety of housewares out of her hand-dyed and batiked fabric. Her work has been featured in numerous exhibitions and in several publications including the *Fiberarts Design Book 7*. She has designed and written for magazines such as *Quilting Arts* and *Quilting Arts Stitch* as well as the books *Sweater Surgery* (Quarry Books, 2008); *Pretty Little Mini Quilts* (Lark Books, 2009); *Quilts, Baby!* (Lark Books, 2009); and *Pretty Little Pillows* (Lark Books, 2010).

Malka currently lives in Austin, Texas, with her husband, three daughters, one dog, two chinchillas, and a tank full of fish. Visit her blog at http://stitchindye.blogspot.com.

Acknowledgments

A project like this is never the work of one individual. A slew of folks contribute time, effort, and encouragement to transform my vision into reality and I would be remiss if I didn't take this opportunity to thank them. First and foremost, I'd like to acknowledge my editor, Darra Williamson, who has offered her expertise and enthusiasm and without whom I could not have written this book. I also offer my thanks and appreciation to Eileen Paulin and Cathy Risling at Red Lips 4 Courage, and the staff at Lark Books for giving me this opportunity. Thanks to Gregory Case, Sue Hartman, and Tim Manibusan, who contributed to the book both in terms of content and design. Thank you to Karen Martin and Ellen Buckmaster for opening up their homes or businesses to help with the photography. A special thanks—wrapped up in much love—goes to my daughter, Abigail, who worked as my model and is my most devoted fan. Thank you to my older girls, Sarah and Rachel, and my husband, Robert, for your encouragement and help with all the little things that get neglected when you're writing a book.

It's all on www.larkbooks.com

Can't find the materials you need to create a project?
Search our database for craft suppliers & sources for hard-to-find materials.

Got an idea for a book?
Read our book proposal guidelines and contact us.

Want to show off your work?
Browse current calls for entries.

Want to know what new and exciting books we're working on?
Sign up for our free e-newsletter.

Feeling crafty?
Find free, downloadable project directions on the site.

Interested in learning more about the authors, designers & editors who create Lark books?

Index

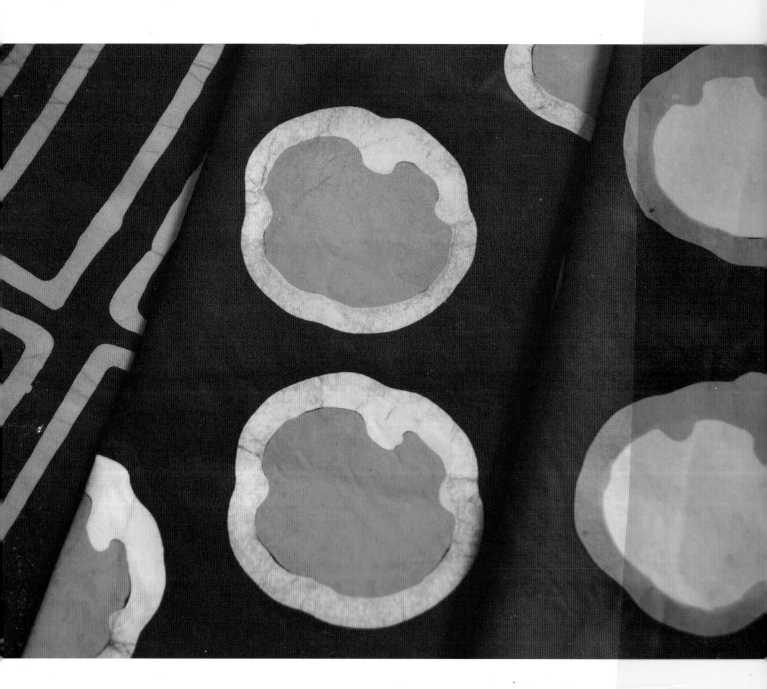